J. ROBERT OPPENHEIMER

J. ROBERT OPPENHEIMER

THE MAN BEHIND THE ATOM BOMB

CHRIS MCNAB

PICTURE CREDITS

Alamy: 7, 82, 167, 174, 197, 200, 205

Wikimedia: 55, 65, 70, 84 (top and bottom), 106, 108, 117, 123, 125 (top and bottom), 132, 136, 145, 147, 150, 156 (top and bottom),168, 172, 173, 181, 206, 209 (top and bottom), 210, 211

This edition published in 2024 by Arcturus Publishing Limited
26/27 Bickels Yard, 151–153 Bermondsey Street,
London SE1 3HA

AD011615UK

Printed in the UK

MIX
Paper | Supporting
responsible forestry
FSC® C171272
www.fsc.org

CONTENTS

INTRODUCTION

As a young man, Oppenheimer stood out both physically and intellectually.

The year was 1965. J. Robert Oppenheimer, the man who became known to popular history as the 'father of the atomic bomb', was then 61 years old. Although he was by no means an old man, the trials of life were nevertheless starting to show. The years had somewhat subdued his character, ironing out much of the Olympian confidence he had exhibited in earlier times. His body was also ill at ease. A harsh smoker's cough, the product of decades of chain-smoking, augured the terminal cancer diagnosis that came later that year.

The event was a TV interview, this one in front of the cameras of CBS News, among America's most respected news broadcast channels. By the 1960s, Oppenheimer was something of a media darling, a sage and scientist demanded by print, radio, TV and the lecture circuit. His role in the Manhattan Project, his views upon US–Soviet relations, the soaring brilliance of his scientific and philosophical mind, the dramas of the hostile security hearings of 1954 – all had contrived to make Oppenheimer the world's most prominent living scientist (the great Albert Einstein had died back in 1955). The press, and the public, seemed to have a bottomless appetite for Oppenheimer's life and work.

One particular question, packaged in various different ways but the same in essence, came back repeatedly. Indeed, it top-ended this interview: 'Looking back now, do you think that the country's use of the bomb was necessary?' Oppenheimer paused after the question was asked, drawing it in carefully before, equally carefully, releasing his answer:

> I believe that the view, which I learned from many but above all from General Marshall and from Colonel Stimson the Secretary of War, the view that they had [was] that we would have to fight our way to the main islands and that it would involve a slaughter of Americans and Japanese on a massive scale. [It] was arrived at by them in good faith, with regret, and on the best evidence that they then had. To that alternative I think the bomb was an enormous relief. The war had started in '39. It had seen the deaths of tens of millions. It had seen brutality and degradation which had no place in the middle of the 20th century. And the ending of the war by this means, certainly cruel, was not undertaken lightly. But I am not, as of today, confident that a better course was then open. I have not a very good answer to this question. [...] I think that when you play a meaningful part in bringing about the death of over a hundred thousand people and the injury of a comparable number you naturally don't think of that with ease.[1]

Oppenheimer handles the question with a perfectly logical justification, laying out the chain of thought that led to the bombings of Hiroshima and Nagasaki in August 1945. But what is telling here is that Oppenheimer follows it up with the equivocal: 'I have not a very good answer to this question.' The final sentence, furthermore, hints that the outcome of the Manhattan Project was so consequentially grave, so hideous to humanity regardless of strategic justification, that Oppenheimer struggled to find ultimate peace with his role in it. The fact that his very loyalty to the USA was later so profoundly, and prominently, questioned (despite evasions that his loyalty was actually *never* in question), can only have compounded his uncertainty. At the very least, his rough handling by the US administration led him to question the judgement and predictability of his nation's political overlords, the very men now in charge of the protean firepower that Oppenheimer had helped to create.

Both psychologically and biographically, the synecdochic mushroom cloud never entirely cleared from Oppenheimer's skies. Oppenheimer held one of the most consequential job roles in modern history – director of the Manhattan Project's Los Alamos Laboratory, the scientific hub responsible for the design, development and production of the atomic bomb. The first two operational bombs vaporized two Japanese cities in milliseconds, searing events that resulted in the immediate or subsequent deaths of some 200,000 people. It was never going to be a role that people would forget or cease to question.

This biography aims to set the 'Los Alamos Years' in their fuller context. For Oppenheimer's 65 years of life should not be judged entirely by the three years he spent working on atomic bombs in a remote desert base, or by the two months of his security hearings in 1954. For a start, we can point to the fact that Oppenheimer was literally one of a cast of thousands involved in developing atomic weaponry. The Manhattan Project eventually swelled to provide employment for at least 130,000 people, including some of the greatest scientists of the 20th century – luminaries such as Leo Szilard, Ernest O. Lawrence, Hans Bethe, Edward Teller, James Chadwick, Robert Serber and Enrico Fermi. The atomic bomb was a very, very long way from being Oppenheimer's unilateral invention. Rather, as director he tended the scientific soil in which the project grew. Nevertheless, he more than anyone was identified as the man who gave the world the reality and threat of atomic destruction, his famous 'pork-pie' hat becoming something of a metonym for the Manhattan Project. Oppenheimer's ultimate problem was a rare one among theoretical physicists. Scientific theory often presents itself in the realm of ideas only, going no further than words, equations and graphs, animated discussions. For Oppenheimer, however, the physics he fostered at Los Alamos had the most profound real-world consequences imaginable, blackboard mathematics converted into twisted railway sleepers, melted glass and mortal ash.

But we should not forget that Oppenheimer was a scientist first, and of the highest order. His work in this domain cannot and should not be tightly bordered purely by his work on atomic weaponry. As we shall see, Oppenheimer also made seminal contributions to physics, plumbing the theoretical depths of cosmic rays and neutron stars, and predicting what we now know as black holes. Oppenheimer was a man of enormous intellectual reach, his mental universe expanding well beyond science into literature, religion, philosophy, art. He was a highly skilled yachtsman and an able horse rider. He was also a man capable of deep oscillations of character and morality, with the capacity for being as unpleasant and vague as he could be urbane and precise.

Writing about Oppenheimer has to acknowledge the surge of public interest in the man following the release of Christopher Nolan's 2023 biographical film *Oppenheimer,* the eponymous title role played with subtle brilliance by Irish actor Cillian Murphy. The film creatively places the spotlight on three of Oppenheimer's great moral struggles: his relationship with Jean Tatlock, the woman with whom he had an affair; his moral compunctions over the development and deployment of the atomic bomb; and his battles with the Atomic Energy Commission (AEC) in the 1950s. It is debatable whether the film fully captures the complexities of Oppenheimer's character. Oppenheimer is neither hero nor villain, but rather a man whose brilliance had a magnetism all of its own, even if he ultimately struggled to wipe all traces of radioactive ash from his jacket sleeves.

CHAPTER 1

THE NEW AMERICAN

Oppenheimer's full name was J. Robert Oppenheimer. According to the balance of research, the initial letter of his name actually did not stand as an abbreviation of anything in particular. Oppenheimer himself stated that the letter represented 'nothing'. His brother Frank was a little more specific, confirming that the letter did not have a definitive expansion, but was rather a respectful nod to their father, Julius, without Robert adopting that name. Regardless, the use of the 'J.' certainly gave Oppenheimer's name a stylish ring, and such, as we shall see, was important in the Oppenheimer family.

The 'Oppenheimer' surname derived from the small town of Oppenheim, located in the Rhenish Hesse region of south-western Germany between Mainz and Worms. The conversion of place to surname came shortly after 20 July 1808, when an imperial degree of the all-conquering Napoleon Bonaparte compelled the Jews of French-occupied territories to take surnames or first names, if they did not possess them already. Many of the German–Jewish community around Oppenheim simply adopted their town's name. Although Robert Oppenheimer's ancestry was firmly Jewish, his relationship to that cultural identity, as we shall see, was not completely comfortable. Indeed, it may well be that the opaque 'J.' in his name was indeed a clear reference to his father, but with the full name hidden because of the contemporary associations of 'Julius' with the Jewish community.

THE NEW YORK OPPENHEIMERS

Julius Oppenheimer was born in the city of Hanau in 1871. While some members of Oppenheimer's extended family would remain rooted in Germany, others joined the mass exodus from Europe to the USA in the 19th century. Julius was one of them, leaving Germany for the promise of America in 1888 at the age of 17. He had a head start in his life as an immigrant, since two of his uncles – Solomon and Sigmund Rothfeld – had emigrated to the USA back in 1869, establishing a highly successful tailoring business in New York. On Julius' arrival, he was greeted by employment in the family firm. The Oppenheimer family interest in New York expanded with the arrival of Julius' brother Emil in 1895.

Despite the tough economic conditions prevailing over the cloth trade in America in the late 19th century, Julius thrived, showing himself to be an astute entrepreneur and businessman. In 1903, he was made a full partner in the company. The year was successful on a personal level too – on 23 March, he married. His bride was Ella Friedman, who was also of German–Jewish ancestry but American-born, already integrated into the American dream.

Julius and Ella formed the two poles between which J. Robert Oppenheimer's character was formed. By all accounts, Julius was gregarious, affable and socially energetic, although his bonhomie appears touched with the insecurity of an immigrant's efforts to fit into a society not of his birth. A friend of Robert Oppenheimer, Robert Horgan, remembered Julius as 'desperately amiable, anxious to be agreeable, and I think essentially a very kind man'.[2] Robert Oppenheimer also acknowledged the essential goodness of his father's character: 'I think my father was one of the most tolerant and human of men. His idea of what to do for people was to let them find out what they wanted.'[3] Fondness for his father, however, would not prevent Oppenheimer junior creating some distance between himself and his parents in later life.

High society has its own unwritten rules and rituals. The slippery subtleties of those codes made entry into that world more than a matter of affluence. Julius certainly sought to avoid any sign of gauche ostentation. One bridge between commercial success and the New York elite was art – Julius became a serious and judicious collector of fine art. He likely met Ella during his visits to New York galleries; she had studied art in Europe and was a capable painter in her own right. Ella was the perfect social balance for Julius. She was refined, elegant, with a dignified reserve. She was also very beautiful. Ella also had a deformed right hand, masked with a prosthetic thumb and forefinger. The early 20th century could be a time insensitive to physical difference, and Ella hid her hand by wearing gloves when in company. Ella's right hand was evidently a touchy family issue, never mentioned nor discussed. Robert was known to respond with icy silence if any outsiders, even close friends or girlfriends, made enquiries about the issue.

Straight after their marriage, Julius and Ella set about creating a family. J. Robert was their first child, entering the world on 22 April 1904. Four years later, in March 1908, Ella gave birth to another son, Lewis Frank Oppenheimer. Tragically, Lewis died just 45 days after his arrival. This event, understandably, cast a pall over the Oppenheimer household, both the family and the physical space in which they lived. Visitors to the Oppenheimer residence sometimes remarked on an aura of melancholy that even Julius' lively personality could not entirely energize.

Perhaps as a byproduct of her bereavement, Ella was particularly anxious for Robert's health and well-being. The early years of his life were rather isolated, Ella seeking to shield her son from the infectious possibilities of other children. The seclusion was occasionally relieved by chauffeur-driven trips out in the countryside beyond the city limits; Robert would grow to have a magnetic pull towards wide-open spaces.

Ella and Julius were blessed with a third son, Frank, on 14 August 1912. Frank Oppenheimer would become one of the closest relationships in Robert Oppenheimer's life, someone who brought out the most relaxed and natural side of his personality. That relationship would, like that with his father, be tested over time.

The Oppenheimers had it good. They lived in finely tuned opulence on the 11th floor apartment at 155 Riverside Drive, New York. It was a highly desirable property in a fashionable neighbourhood. The apartment occupied the entire floor of the building and the windows offered tremendous views out over the Hudson River. Julius' commercial success meant that the Oppenheimers could afford domestic staff, including chauffeurs and maids, but affluence was always tempered by good manners and restrained taste. The family culture was also shaped by broader social changes that had been taking place in the Jewish-American community since the late 19th century.

For many Jewish families in the USA at this time, but especially those who had emigrated from Germany, Jewish culture remained important. But as those families sought to enjoy new lives in America, the traditions and rites had become increasingly overlaid with more secular and integrationist movements. To be separate was not always desirable, particularly for those wanting to drive commercial success and social respect. But making the effort to blend in did not automatically open the doors of American society. The terrifying anti-Semitism of Nazi Germany in the first half of the 20th century can blind us to the deep hostility to Jews that thrived elsewhere, and the USA was no exception. It was not uncommon for Jews to be explicitly or covertly barred from 'elite' spaces – sports and social clubs, universities, high-class hotels, institutional positions. American anti-Semitism ran deep despite the fact that some Jewish-American families had become titans of American business and cultural patronage, august families such as the Roosevelts, Astors, Vanderbilts and Morgans taking keystone roles in building the modern USA. Such was the desire of the Western European Jewish-Americans to promote their modern American identity that many were even opposed to further waves of Jewish immigration from Eastern Europe, fearful that the more religious outlook and devout practices of the new arrivals would act as a lightning rod for growing anti-Semitism.

One of the most prominent movements in Jewish-American secularization was the Ethical Culture Society. This organization had been founded in 1876 by another German-Jewish immigrant, Felix Adler, the son of a rabbi. Adler's philosophical goal was to separate ethical behaviour from the observance of the codes and laws of the great monotheistic faiths, including his own Judaism. He encouraged his adherents to focus their moral efforts on improving their characters and (through education) their intellects, while also promoting a generous, class-conscious altruism and a reformist spirit. The emphasis on activism meant that the educational element of Ethical Culture, its dedicated private schools, became seen as incubators for future American leaders. The movement still had a tangible connection to its Jewish heritage, but its educational and ideological focus was socially open – its school accepted gentiles. In 1911, Robert's world broadened when he began attending the second grade of his local Ethical Culture School in New York. He would thrive in the Ethical Culture environment right through to his high-school graduation.

EDUCATING ROBERT

Oppenheimer doubtless had genetics on his side when it came to his intellect. His emerging ability to remember almost everything that he read after a single pass was a talent that couldn't be acquired by diligence or process. But he also grew up in a world that was making every effort to help him excel, beginning with his parents' earnest desire to ensure his intellectual and social advancement. The Ethical Culture School, with its encouragement of self-identified learning paths, was ideal for the curious young man.

Every flash of attention was encouraged. His early subject interests appear to have been triggered by two visits to Germany, when he was five and seven years old, to meet his paternal grandfather, Benjamin Oppenheimer. In later life, Oppenheimer was interviewed by the American philosopher and historian Thomas Kuhn. During the interview, Oppenheimer described his grandfather as 'an unsuccessful business man, born himself into a hovel, really, in an almost medieval German village [likely Hanau], with a taste for scholarship'.[4] There is a hint of condescension here, but Oppenheimer was nevertheless genuinely grateful towards Grandfather Benjamin on account of two small gifts he received from him: an encyclopaedia of architecture and a small collection of minerals. Robert was apparently absorbed by both, feeding into the exponentially expanding appetite for reading and knowledge. A revealing passage from the Kuhn interview shows Oppenheimer formulating the foundations of his own intellectual development:

From then on I became, in a completely childish way, an ardent mineral collector and I had, by the time I was through, quite a fine collection ... This was certainly at first a collector's interest, but it began to be also a bit of a scientist's interest, not in historical problems of how rocks and minerals came to be, but really a fascination with crystals, their structure, bi-refringence, what you saw in polarised light, and all the canonical business ... When I was ten or twelve years old, minerals, writing poems and reading, and building with blocks still – architecture – were the three themes that I did, not because they were something I had companionship in or because they had any relation to school but just for the hell of it. I gave up the blocks probably at the age of 10, and the minerals became a charming preoccupation. I started trying to understand them. I had very great trouble because I didn't always know the vocabulary; I think it was a month before I realised that 'intercept' could be used as a noun as well as a verb and this was the bane of me.[5]

Oppenheimer describes the first stirrings of a personality trait common to many scientists – the burning, almost painful, compulsion to *know*, to unpack the hidden structures of reality, revealing its laws, properties and mysteries. Oppenheimer is also yearning to acquire to verbal tools of scientific description; throughout his life, he sought a mastery of expression in many linguistic domains, from art and literature to foreign languages and theoretical physics.

A simple box of minerals, therefore, quickly moved from an object of idle curiosity to a new universe of ideas. Certainly, mineralogy become more than a mere hobby. His knowledge of the subject grew to such an extent that he joined the prestigious New York Mineralogical Club, founded in 1886. He was the organization's youngest member, even presenting a paper to the society when he was just 12 years old.

It did not take long for the teachers at the Ethical Culture School to recognize that they had a truly exceptional student on their hands. Oppenheimer clearly stood out from the rest. As he accelerated through the curriculum, he also made some formative connections with a small handful of teachers. Two stand out in particular. First is the English teacher Herbert Winslow Smith, who provided not only responsive intellectual stimulus, but also extended kind-hearted pastoral concern, forging a bond between student and teacher than lasted well beyond Oppenheimer's school years. In 1974, after Oppenheimer's death, Smith gave a lengthy interview to Charles Weiner, in which he offered his perceptive memories of Oppenheimer as man and boy. (A full transcript of this interview is provided online by the Center for History of Physics of the American Institute of Physics – see the Bibliography for details.)

Regarding Oppenheimer's school years, Smith recollected how Oppenheimer felt that his parents' – but particularly his father's – 'maladroitness' was a source of humiliation for the boy. Smith provided evidence to back this claim. One summer, Robert attended a school summer held at Camp Koenig, located on the picturesque 11-acre Grindstone Island on Lake Ontario. Once at the camp, Robert began to draw unwelcome attention from surrounding bullies. He acquired the nickname 'Cutie', on account of what was regarded as a rather effete appearance, with his thick, bushy hair, delicate physical frame, and angular, sensitive features. Without condoning bullying behaviour, it does appear that the young Oppenheimer did his best to paint a target on himself. According to Fred Koenig, the son of camp organizer Dr Otto Koenig and Oppenheimer's only real friend during the camp, Robert conducted himself with a superior air, aware of his own intellectual elevation above the common herd. This only served to increase the predatory animosity. (Oppenheimer's snobbery, as we shall see, was a kind of compound interest running through many of the trials he experienced in later life, making bad situations worse.)

During the camp event, Oppenheimer was exposed to the naturally ribald conversation of young boys. With jejune misreading of his parents, Robert wrote a letter to them cockily saying he was learning a lot about sex. This prompted an angry and fretful impromptu visit to the camp by Julius and Ella, resulting in investigation and castigation all round. Vengeance came one evening. A group of other boys grabbed Robert and dragged him to an isolated icehouse. There they stripped him, tied him up, painted his buttocks and genitals green, and left him alone in humiliation and fear for some time.

We know that this incident was traumatic to Oppenheimer because he only revealed its occurrence when he was 20 years old, telling his confidant Herbert Smith. Julius and Ella's (mis)handling of the incident, Smith explained, illustrates the awkward relationship between son and parents. Oppenheimer's combined affection for and embarrassment of his parents became something of a recurrent theme, especially as he went into his university years.

He saw his father in particular as somewhat crude and unpolished, displaying the trait the upper classes could spot in an instant – the desperate desire to fit in among one's 'betters'.

Another individual who would make a lasting impression on Oppenheimer at the Ethical Culture School was Augustus Klock, a science teacher. Frank Oppenheimer's memories of Klock were less than reverential, noting that Klock taught physics 'with some excitement' but that his instruction in chemistry was generally uninspiring. Robert Oppenheimer, by contrast, eulogized 'Gus' Klock in a remembrance following the teacher's death in 1963:

> It is almost forty-five years since Augustus Klock taught me physics and chemistry ... He loved these sciences both as craft and knowledge. He loved the devices of the laboratory, and the great discoveries that had been made before, and the view of nature – part order, part puzzle, that is the condition of science. But above all, he loved young people, to whom he hoped to give some touch, some taste, some love of life, and in whose awakening he saw his destiny.[6]

It is interesting that Oppenheimer here focuses on the fusion of theory and practice as Klock's inspirational gift. In his later academic and professional life, Oppenheimer gravitated towards theoretical physics, struggling with the practical engineering demands that came with experimental physics. But clearly Klock's enthusiasm for the apparatus, ideas and quest of science was transferred to Oppenheimer. While in no way downplaying the seriousness of Oppenheimer's work at Los Alamos, we should not underestimate the sheer thrill of many great minds, supported by an unlimited budget, gathering in one place to pursue the ultimate expression of practical physics.

As much as Klock inspired Oppenheimer, in return Oppenheimer was the type of engaged student, full of unbridled potential, whom Klock adored. On 8 November 1948, *Time* magazine published an article entitled 'The Eternal Apprentice', a long reflection on Oppenheimer's intellectual and vocational journey. (Indicative of the fame Oppenheimer had achieved by this stage, the cover of the magazine issue was a full-colour portrait of Oppenheimer.) The article reflects on the exceptional nature of Oppenheimer's educational beginnings, observing that by the time Oppenheimer graduated from the Ethical Culture School he 'could read Caesar, Virgil and Horace without a Latin dictionary, had read Plato and Homer in the Greek, composed sonnets in French and tackled treatises on polarized light'. [7] The cognitive breadth here reminds us that although Oppenheimer is primarily revered as a scientist, he was a true polymath, aided by his exceptional memory. (The one subject for which he never appeared to demonstrate either ability or interest, at least in childhood, was music.) The article also quotes Klock, who saw Oppenheimer's intellectual ascent as irresistible: 'He was so brilliant that no teacher would have been skilful enough to prevent him from getting an education.' [8]

Looking back upon his childhood, Oppenheimer recognized that he was a rather pampered and sheltered boy, in need of toughening up: 'My life as a child did not prepare me for the fact that the world is full of cruel and bitter things.' His affluent surroundings and overly attentive parents meant that he (here with Oppenheimer's gift for a memorable phrase), 'found no normal, healthy way to be a bastard'. [9] But he did forge a select group of friends, of both sexes. One was classmate Jane Didisheim. Jane was enough of a friend to spend time at Robert's home; her visits were encouraged by Ella, who saw in Jane a potential future mate for her sensitive son, or at least someone who might draw him out of his shell.[10]

It does seem that Robert held Jane in romantic regard, and his affection for her extended into his university years. Any yearnings, however, were not reciprocated. In later life, Jane (now Jane Kayser) remembered the young Oppenheimer tenderly, but spotlighted the deeply entrenched awkwardness of the boy, especially in terms of his physical mannerisms.

She noted that he was small in stature, and 'very frail', with especially bright pink cheeks. In fact, Jane saw Robert as 'rather undeveloped', a state expressed itself through physical awkwardness in posture and movement. These characteristics were compounded by a tendency towards shyness. But when it came to the intellectual domain, she observed, Robert was clearly superior to those around him, something that his peer group were quick to recognize. It was not just that he was fast at acquiring and processing knowledge, but that he was also adept at all subjects, from the artistic to the scientific.[11]

Oppenheimer's delicate physique is confirmed by many other sources. At one point, his aversion to exertion of any description meant that he even went to some lengths to avoid using stairs. The challenges this created led to the school headmaster writing to Ella and Julius, asking them to encourage their son to start using stairs as a matter of course.

Kayser's portrait of Oppenheimer makes clear why young romance didn't take hold, but she acknowledges his superior intellectual powers. Generally, he was a shy boy, keeping to the back of the room, but on occasions his knowledge would propel him to take centre stage at the front of the class 'because he was so extraordinarily gifted and brilliant'.[12]

Other close associates from his high-school years included a younger boy named Fred Bernheim and two sisters, Inez and Kitty Pollak. But by far the greatest of his friends, a lifelong confidant, was Francis Fergusson. Many biographers of Oppenheimer explore the extent to which Fergusson was not merely Oppenheimer's friend, but also a model of behaviour and breeding to which Oppenheimer aspired. Fergusson hailed from Albuquerque, New Mexico, the son of a state Congressman. He attended the Ethical Culture School for only one year, between 1920 and 1921, but it coincided with Oppenheimer's senior year.

Fergusson shared intellectual prowess with Oppenheimer. His metier at school was writing and philosophy. (He would maintain this direction into adulthood, building a career as a teacher, literary critic and also a specialist in theatre and mythology.) Oppenheimer and Fergusson were doubtless drawn to each other as fellow polymaths. But in many other ways, the gentile Fergusson was quite different to his New Yorker, Jewish friend. Fergusson was confident and sharp, but also carried what for Oppenheimer was the frontier spirit of the American Southwest, a ruggedness in thought and deed imparted by an inspiring and untamed wilderness. This profile sat in contrast to Oppenheimer's protected sensitivity, his urban fragility. The young are defined by a pressing desire to conform to the optimal norm and are easily inspired by anyone who they think has somehow cracked the social code. In Fergusson, Oppenheimer saw someone who merged effortlessly into the elite of society, while Oppenheimer himself felt that his own character and culture were things to conceal. Herbert Smith remembers this tendency in Oppenheimer: 'Well he had really grown up believing that it was a shame, a sort of thing that you were born with and never got over, to belong to the Jewish group.'[13] Oppenheimer's struggles with his own Jewish background would run for many years into his adulthood.

BREAKING OUT

By the time Oppenheimer reached the end of his senior year he had forged a small, tight group of friends. He was also beginning to discover the outdoors. The break point came on his 16th birthday, when Julius – evidently wanting to help his son discover a more adventurous spirit – bought him an 8.2 m (27 ft) sloop. The Oppenheimer family had another residence in the picturesque coastal hamlet of Bay Sound, in Suffolk County, Long Island. The property had an anchorage that provided easy access to the waters of Long Island Sound and the Great South Bay. Given that Robert's aversion to physical pursuits extended to the use of stairs, it could have been a gift that fell spectacularly flat. Instead, it ignited a passion for sailing that would help transform him both mentally and physically.

Robert named the boat *Trimethy*, a knowing play on the chemical compound trimethylamine, which is responsible for the familiar coastal smell of rotting fish. Together, Frank and Robert spent countless hours on the boat, cementing their brotherly bond while turning them into proficient sailors. Robert also discovered a latent appetite for pushing the boundaries of risk-taking, launching the boat into hostile, choppy weather, much to the concern of his parents. The adventures sometimes went too far; the boys had to be recovered from distant parts of the coastline on several occasions by Julius, and there was even a Coast Guard rescue required when the boat ran aground on a mud bank. Fergusson, who was taken out on the water in rough conditions, remembered being genuinely scared, but impressed by Robert's handling of the craft. He also noted Ella's helpless anxiety over her son's new-found desire for peril.

In the spring of 1921, Oppenheimer graduated from the Ethical Culture School. He, along with Fergusson, was heading to Harvard University – then, as now, one of the elite educational institutions in the USA. Oppenheimer was intending to study chemistry. A summer break separated school from university. Robert spent the immediate months after graduation working on a science project with Augustus Klock. That completed, he next enjoyed a trip to Europe with his family. While the family were in Germany, Robert indulged his interest in mineralogy by visiting the mines at Joachimsthal in Bohemia (today Jáchymov) on the German–Czech border. Ore mining at Joachimsthal dated back to the 16th century, first in the extraction of silver ore but later expanding to include nickel, bismuth, lead, arsenic, cobalt, tin, uranium and radium. Oppenheimer found much to appreciate in the mines and also took the opportunity to expand his growing personal collection of mineral rocks. But one truly unwelcome takeaway from the mines was that he contracted dysentery.

His illness was no minor ailment – it became genuinely life-threatening. Back in the USA, seriously ill, Robert was forced to postpone his admission to Harvard that year, it being apparent that the return to full health would be a long and painful journey. Although he did recover from dysentery, the illness left him with lifelong colitis (a swelling or inflammation of the large intestine).

This condition made his relationship with spicy food (which he loved) problematic, while also contributing to a sporadic grumpiness and irritability.

The pre-Harvard period of illness was a mental struggle as well as a physical one. Robert slumped into a melancholy funk, locking himself in his room and refusing to come out, regardless of his parents' anxious pleas. But the clouds of illness would ultimately break to reveal a silver lining. In a successful attempt to draw him out of his depression, Julius and Ella asked Herbert Smith if he would take Robert on a trip to the American Southwest, offering to cover Smith's salary while he did so. Smith's extra-curricular care for his students was not unprecedented. He was known to invite promising young students to meetings and trips, generous with his time and energy and keen for their advancement. He agreed to the plan for young Robert, who also appeared to embrace the continental voyage with enthusiasm.

The destination was New Mexico, not least because it gave both Smith and Oppenheimer the opportunity to visit Fergusson and meet his family. On the whole, the trip had a transformative effect on Oppenheimer, changing his vision of his country and his potential place in it. But it would also give Smith the opportunity to observe Oppenheimer more closely, on the cusp of adulthood. He noted again Oppenheimer's prickly sensitivity to his Jewish background. For example, during the planning phase for the trip Oppenheimer made the suggestion that he and Smith actually pretend to be brothers, with Oppenheimer taking Smith's surname if asked, especially when meeting new people or checking into hotels. Smith wisely refused. But Oppenheimer also proved sensitive to what he saw as Jewish associations. Smith remembered one uncomfortable incident:

I remember, we were packing to go—I've never been able to pack
a coat so it would look like anything when I took it out. And he,
that was one thing he had down to perfection. And I said, because
we were rushing, I said, 'Can you make this coat fold up so it's
not looking like anything?' He looked at me sharply and said, 'Oh
yes—the tailor's son would know how to do that, wouldn't he?'[14]

At this time in history, Jews (and especially German Jews) were
often identified with the American tailoring industry; unions such
as the International Ladies' Garment Workers' Union and the
Amalgamated Clothing Workers of America (ACW) had a strong
Jewish presence among their leadership. So, Oppenheimer was
likely seeing a metonymic slight, a connection between tailoring
and his Jewish ancestry. Even if the offence taken was not so cul-
turally layered, Oppenheimer was obviously piqued at being associated with the world of 'trades'.

Such moments aside, however, Oppenheimer's journey to and
through New Mexico brought far more relief than tension. His
visit to the Fergusson home was a revelation. There Oppenheimer
found a family imbued with a distinctly American form of assur-
ance, replete with the confidence of self and place that he sought for
himself. The Fergussons were cultured, outgoing and discursive,
but also hardy and altruistic, their home that enigmatic fusion of
Spanish and American, of easy wealth and simple antiquity. There
was a youthful buzz, Oppenheimer being introduced to new faces.
One of them was Paul Horgan, a friend of Francis who originated
from Buffalo, New York, but whose family had settled in Albuquerque. Horgan, as with so many of Oppenheimer's friends, was
destined for greatness: in later life he became a renowned writer

and historian, publishing more than 40 books, receiving 19 honorary degrees and winning a Pulitzer Prize. But back in 1922, he was a student at the New Mexico Military Institute.

Despite differing academic interests, Oppenheimer, Fergusson and Horgan were united by their advanced polymathic intellects. Oppenheimer was destined to make his mark in science, but his interests were broad and voracious, so the three young men found plenty of ground for the exchange of ideas. The summer of 1922 bonded them firmly as a friendship group. Horgan later referred to them affectionately as the 'great troika' or 'pygmy triumvirate'.

Given later events in Oppenheimer's life, it is interesting that Horgan labelled the group using the Russian word *troika*, more commonly applied to a Soviet triumvirate. In May 1922, Vladimir Lenin, the leader of the Bolshevik/Communist Party in revolutionary Russia, suffered a stroke. To maintain leadership, a temporary troika was formed to rule in his stead, consisted of Lev Kamenev, Grigory Zinoviev and none other than Joseph Stalin. By the time the three young Americans were forging summery memories in New Mexico, the Soviet Union had not even reached its formal creation (that would come on 30 December 1922), but the Bolsheviks had clearly consolidated victory and control. Being generally well-informed boys, Oppenheimer and his friends would likely be aware of this, and certainly of the communist ideas that had been taking root in parts of American trade and culture since the 19th century. The Communist Party of the United States of America (CPUSA) had been formed in 1919, with just over 12,000 members nationwide by 1922. I am not, by any means, here searching for a neat foundation story to explain the later problems Oppenheimer had on account of his real and fictional relationships with communism. However, Horgan's use of the word *troika* might suggest that the boys at least regarded communism with a stirring romanticism, as many in the Western hemisphere did in the early decades of the Soviet Union.

Any ideological awakenings, however, likely paled when compared to Oppenheimer's stirring interest in the opposite sex. As part of the trip, Oppenheimer went to stay at the Los Pinos guest ranch, located in the Upper Pecos Valley, Sangre de Cristo Mountains, near the hamlet of Cowles. The ranch was run by two friends of the Fergussons, husband and wife team Winthrop and Katherine Chaves Page. There was a major age difference between the two. Winthrop was in his 50s, but Katherine was just 28, and an attractive figure in both appearance and character. She was of Spanish aristocratic stock, her family's history an epic forged from war, exploration, courage, politics and leadership, all played out against the backdrop of a protean nation. In herself, Katherine was self-possessed and resilient, at home in both her history and the dusty New Mexican wilderness.

Oppenheimer appears hopelessly, understandably, attracted towards Katherine. He started bringing her flowers with slightly obsessive regularity. It even appears that the highest lake in New Mexico, Lake Katherine (3,580 m/11,745 ft elevation) on Sante Fe Baldy, was named after Katherine and not, as sometimes suggested, after his future wife. While the romantic efforts were naturally not reciprocated, Katherine does not appear to have dissuaded the earnest attentions of Oppenheimer's first grown-up crush.

The relationship between Katherine and Robert may have been a one-sided and impossible longing, but it had an important practical outcome for Oppenheimer. At Los Pinos, Oppenheimer learned how to ride. As with sailing, he acquired the skill with instinctive intelligence, and showed genuine ability quickly. Thus it was often on horseback that Oppenheimer and his group of friends explored the New Mexican wilderness, which can only have added to the Old World romanticism of the experience.

It is hard to overstate the psychological impact New Mexico had on Oppenheimer. Its bush-covered mountains, hoof-worn trails, wind-blown plateaus, hardy and cruel wildlife – all spoke of a frontier freedom and a nobility and toughness of character, free from the petty concerns of the city. It was a place that for Oppenheimer encouraged thought as expansive as the horizons. He became a true lover of the great outdoors, whether hiking, sailing or riding. His friends were also noticing a difference in his character. Jane Didisheim felt that he was becoming 'less shy', his self-assurance swelled by his sense of belonging to a group of friends with a shared experience. Herbert Smith also picked up on this shift: 'So this was the first time in his life that Robert found himself loved, admired, sought after.'[15]

The gravitational pull of New Mexico on Oppenheimer's psyche would remain irresistible. Just a few years later, he would say: 'My two great loves are physics and New Mexico. It's a pity they can't be combined.'[16] He could not have conceived how wrong that last sentence could be.

CHAPTER 2

STRUGGLING TO THINK: FROM HARVARD TO GÖTTINGEN

Biographers of J. Robert Oppenheimer have the good fortune that he left a large repository of letters from his life. (Many of the most important were diligently gathered in a single volume: Alice Kimball Smith and Charles Weiner's *Robert Oppenheimer: Letters and Recollections* – see Bibliography.) They were sent to friends, family, colleagues, journalists, correspondents, officials, even presidents. They range from the intimate and confessional to the guarded and defensive. Those he wrote during his undergraduate years at Harvard University (1922–25), and in his subsequent study periods in the UK and Germany, often make for strange reading.

AT AN ANGLE

Undergraduate pretension is common, but Oppenheimer's letters to Fergusson, Smith and others take the desire to impress to whole new levels of effort and, at times, awkwardness. Profiled psychologically, the letters seem compelled by a mutually antagonistic combination of superiority and insecurity, despite the leaps in self-assurance made in the previous chapter. Here is just a thin slice, from a letter written to Fergusson on 16 August 1923:

At last I see an opportunity for one of those longwinded, tapestried apologies whose prospect always delights me. Think of the august and pompous genuflections with which I might open this letter; consider the glittering array of explanations, the platoons of excuses, the phalanxes of apologetics that I might marshal to salute you. Racine himself could have conceived no more melodramatic a situation, nor one more prolific of potential sonorous verbalisms: – It is ten days since your letter arrived. – Thus long have I delayed an answer, thus brazenly have I neglected to thank you – Hélas.[17]

Even allowing for a degree of self-mockery, it is hard to see the authentic Oppenheimer in this passage, rather a polished and interleaved imitation of conventions, references and knowing allusions.

Looking across the breadth of his letters from this period, we see repeatedly Oppenheimer's deep desire to *belong*, fearing cultural and intellectual exclusion above all things. Seen superficially, we might wonder why Oppenheimer felt such anxiety when, between 1922 and 1927, he was accepted into three of the world's most lauded educational institutions: Harvard, Cambridge and Göttingen, beginning as an undergraduate student in chemistry and emerging with a PhD in theoretical physics, gathering the respect of international peers along the way. But while higher education clarified intellectual direction, some of his deep-seated insecurities remained unresolved. In fact, his university years were often a time of loneliness, insecurity and hypochondria, culminating in what can only be defined as full-blown episodes of mental breakdown. He remained a difficult person to know and, often, even to like. Oppenheimer could be snide, disloyal, critical and unpleasant, with towering arrogance. But self-loathing underpinned much of his disdain, and was spotted by those closest to him. His hidden shadows were perhaps best summed up in 1974 by Jane Kayser (formerly Didisheim) in correspondence with Herbert Smith, relating to Oppenheimer's early romantic letters to her. She told Smith that he ought to add the word 'vulnerable' to the adjectives that he used to describe Oppenheimer. With a clear sense of regret, she confessed that she must have been 'callous' not to have seen the fragile, sensitive attachment Oppenheimer had towards her in those early days, and how 'thin-skinned' he was at an emotional level.[18]

HARVARD

Oppenheimer entered Harvard in 1922. The year was significant for someone of his background. That very year, the longstanding president of Harvard University – Abbott Lawrence Lowell – was actively and openly pushing to reduce the intake of Jewish students, restricting the Jewish enrolment to 15 per cent of the total student body (at the time, it was at 22 per cent). Although Lowell presented this measure as an equity policy, it naturally drummed up controversy, given the context of widespread anti-Semitism in the USA then current. Although direct restrictions on Jewish intake were not adopted, more indirect measures still achieved what Lowell set out to do – by the time he left the office in 1933, Jews represented just 10 per cent of the student cohort. Notably, in his extant letters Oppenheimer does not comment on this situation. We might speculate that acknowledging the issue might, in Oppenheimer's mind, actually reinforce his sense of cultural separateness. Whatever the case, it is difficult to think that he wasn't aware of the debate around Jewish attendance of Harvard in the summer of 1922.

Oppenheimer took up residence in the Standish Hall dormitory, Room D 12. As was customary for a freshman, he pursued a broad sweep of courses that crossed the sciences and the humanities, specifically:

Elementary Organic Chemistry
Rhetoric and English Composition
Qualitative Analysis
French Prose and Poetry, Corneille through Zola
Analytic Geometry and Introduction to Calculus
History of Philosophy

Apparently, there were strategies that could be employed to opt out of those courses the student deemed non-essential to their intellectual development. But Oppenheimer both failed to discover them and, more to the point, embraced the polymathic curriculum. In addition to his love of science, Oppenheimer had a genuine passion for literature and ideas, plus a broad cultural knowledge was a necessary marker of the man of letters. Throughout his academic career, therefore, Oppenheimer voraciously read and digested works not on the university reading lists. His Herculean memory meant that each book swelled his intellectual power like a muscle in a gym. And he was keen to show the breadth of his learning – his aforementioned letters are littered with urbane cultural references.

At Harvard, Oppenheimer also made some attempts at writing fiction, principally in the form of short stories. The themes of these stories have been the subject of some amateur psychoanalysis, as biographers use them to open windows on preoccupations and battles within Oppenheimer's mind. For example, in January

1923 Oppenheimer explained to Smith that he was composing a tale about a mining engineer, which was actually a career that Oppenheimer was then seriously contemplating. In the story, the engineer is caught between being intellectually superior to those around him, while at the same time feeling intensely vulnerable. He initially despises the rough-hewn miners, but eventually grows to understand and embrace them once he has negotiated his own insecurities. Given what we know about this period of his life, the autobiographical elements of this story seem hard to deny.

Socially, Harvard brought both new horizons and the deepening of some existing friendships. Fergusson was already there, beginning his sophomore year. This meant that Oppenheimer had a ready friend on arrival, but soon Fergusson secured a prestigious Rhodes Scholarship at Cambridge University, so moved to the UK. Oppenheimer already held Fergusson in elevated regard, but his friend's transition to Cambridge took that veneration to even greater altitude. The letters Oppenheimer wrote to Fergusson are at times both sycophantic and defensive (in addition to being genuinely affectionate), especially when Oppenheimer compares his literary efforts with those produced by his capable friend. A protective adoption of inferiority comes through in the following example: 'I suppose it is never quite possible for us to understand each other's layers of naiveté. And it is that which keeps [me] from agreeing with entirely what you say about the junk I send you. I think all the snarkiest things you say – and by the way, thank you for troubling – are perfectly true.'[19] Oppenheimer condemns his outputs as 'junk', at least comparatively, and further down acknowledges his 'dilettante dawdling in literature'. It is difficult to know whether there is false humility here, but certainly Oppenheimer's experiments with fiction writing remained just that – experiments – while Fergusson went on to be enormously respected for his work in literature. The tension that is evident in what is a particularly long letter perhaps makes it more understandable when Oppenheimer appears to have then taken an 18-month break in his letter-writing to Fergusson.

Harvard also brought the opportunity for new friendships. A salient figure for Oppenheimer was the aforementioned Fred Bernheim. He was also a graduate of the Ethical Culture School but had been a year behind Oppenheimer; Robert's illness-induced hiatus in 1921–22 meant that they both arrived at Harvard in the same semester. Their friendship intensified at Harvard, cemented by their being roommates in Standish Hall; they also shared an off-campus apartment in their sophomore year.

Many people at Harvard sensed a hint of lip-curling arrogance in Oppenheimer. Bernheim was aware of this trait (others told him so), which could be hard work for him too: 'He wasn't a comfortable person to be around, in a way, because he always gave the impression that he was thinking very deeply about things.'[20] Bernheim was also clear-sighted about Oppenheimer's frequent pretentiousness, especially when he punctuated his sentences with arcane French quotations.

But Oppenheimer's aloofness did not, at first, erect an insurmountable barrier between them. They were both super-bright and shared the same punishing work ethic. Oppenheimer also found rare scraps of spare time to sit down with Bernheim for tea and pleasant discussions. But one trait of Oppenheimer's that was problematic was his tendency to become obsessional and possessive over Bernheim's friends. Oppenheimer took exception to Bernheim meeting and introducing new people, apparently hostile to the thought of Bernheim forging parallel friendships. Similarly, he also became brittle towards Bernheim dating girls, as if by seeing females Bernheim was pursuing an inevitable conflict of interest.

Over time, Oppenheimer's controlling attitude towards Bernheim (and Bernheim's refusal to bow to it) became unsustainable for their friendship. After they graduated from Harvard in 1925, both subsequently continued their studies in Cambridge, although the separate housing related to their courses meant that they were not living close to each other. Bernheim eventually had enough. The friendship was effectively shut down over a lavish English high tea, during which Bernheim told Oppenheimer that going forward he didn't really have the spare time to devote to sustaining a close friendship.

But winding back to the halcyon days of Harvard, for a time Bernheim and Oppenheimer were inseparable. When not in college, the pair would head off for the weekend to the pleasant and affluent peninsula of Cape Ann in northern Massachusetts. They soon added another spoke to the wheel in the form of fellow chemistry student William Clouser Boyd from Missouri (often referred to by Oppenheimer in his writings as 'Clowser'.) Boyd judged Oppenheimer as 'a very talented person, very able and very sensitive'.[21] He found Oppenheimer's complete lack of interest in all forms of music puzzling, however.

Together, Oppenheimer, Bernheim and Boyd formed what Bernheim described as a 'unit', effectively another friendship *troika*. Bernheim and Boyd were a stolid support for Oppenheimer's brittle ego during the Harvard years. Later, Oppenheimer also befriended Jeffries Wyman, a biology graduate student from Boston. Wyman was reliably impressed with Oppenheimer's intelligence, but they also shared off-campus fun.

And what of romance? While university for many is where first serious relationships are forged, for Oppenheimer the female students offered some occasional distraction and attraction. But by all accounts he was too absorbed in his studies and too self-conscious to pursue college girls.

Beyond his circle of friends, Oppenheimer's involvement with the broader social and cultural life of Harvard was limited. In the early days at university he made a connection with another student called Algernon Black. He was yet another from the Ethical Culture School stable, and at Harvard he became a spokesman for the recently formed Liberal Club. Unlike many of the clubs on campus, the Liberal Club was open to Jews. Another club member was chemistry student John Edsall, and it was he who recognized that Oppenheimer's astonishing mind might be put to good use. He invited Oppenheimer to work on the Liberal Club's fledgling journal, which was so nascent that it didn't even have a title. Showing his instant value, Oppenheimer solved this problem by suggesting *The Gad-Fly*, playing on the sense of one who upsets the status quo. Oppenheimer helped out on the first two issues of the newly named journal, but then dropped away from club involvement. Throughout his university years, Oppenheimer would show little interest in politics – that would come later.

Oppenheimer did give his time to a small science discussion group founded by Fergusson, among others. The basic format of the group was to invite a professor to a cosy room, listen to him present an idea or paper, then discuss. It would have been a close-knit forum to Oppenheimer's liking, both for its intellectual stimulus and for his opportunity to shine.

The most important academic development for Oppenheimer at Harvard was his progressive shift into the world of theoretical physics. Oppenheimer had never observed hard frontiers between chemistry and physics, seeing both as in continual interplay. But at Harvard, he began reading theoretical physics works enthusiastically. Even on sailing trips, his friends would often note that Oppenheimer sat with a new physics tome in hand. Works such as James Jeans' *The Mathematical Theory of Electricity and Magnetism* laid some of the essential theoretical groundwork, but he then fearlessly plunged into the most advanced content he could find.

Oppenheimer's confidence and interest in physics grew to such an extent that on 24 May 1923 he wrote a letter to the university's only theoretical physicist, Edwin C. Kemble, asking to be accepted on to the Physics 6a course on thermodynamics. This was a bold request, partly because of the potential increase in his workload, but also because Physics 6a was a *graduate* course, attended by students who had already completed their first degrees. Note that by this stage Oppenheimer had not even attended a single *undergraduate* physics course.

To convince Kemble, Oppenheimer laid out his academic credentials and the strength of his self-learning. To show that his mind was capable of stepping into graduate physics, he also listed some of the works he had read and absorbed. They included G.N. Lewis and M. Randall's *Thermodynamics*; J.W. Gibbs' *On the Equilibrium of Heterogeneous Gases*; Walther Nernst's *Thermodynamics and Chemistry* and Arnold Sommerfeld's *Atombau und Spectral-linien*, four among a longer list that Oppenheimer contextualized as a 'partial list'. Monk notes that some errors in the bibliographic information suggest that Oppenheimer might not have been totally familiar with all of the books on his list, but no matter – sheer front paid off. So Oppenheimer was accepted into the graduate course, beginning it in his second year of study.

Oppenheimer was ambitiously aiming to graduate in three years, instead of the customary four. This yielded a formidable workload. In his second year at Harvard, Oppenheimer was studying three chemistry modules, two mathematics modules, three physics modules, one philosophy module and one French literature module, spread over the spring and fall semesters. According to his own later admission, the scale of the programme he willingly embraced meant that some balls were dropped, at least by his own standards – in two of his courses, he received B grades instead of A grades. Nevertheless, in 1925 Oppenheimer graduated with an AB summa cum laude in chemistry. He didn't ultimately attend his own graduation ceremony; instead he retired to Bernheim's room and the two men got drunk together on lab alcohol.

CAMBRIDGE BLUES

The first two decades of the 20th century transformed physics, comparable to the leaps taken by the likes of Galileo, Pascal, Boyle, Huygens and Newton in the 17th century. Most popularly known are Albert Einstein's theories of special and general relativity. In 1905, Einstein explained special relativity through his paper 'On the Electrodynamics of Moving Bodies', remodelling our fundamental understanding of the relationship between space and time, and between energy and matter. In 1915 he laid the groundwork for much modern theoretical physics through general relativity, in which he mathematically delineated the curvature of spacetime, the indistinguishability of gravity and acceleration, and gravitational time dilation – theories later proven experimentally. With Einstein, physics began its breakaway from the classical models of the past, challenging our notions about the constitution of reality itself.

But Einstein was just one of the pioneers around this time, especially in the context of a new branch of theory known at first as 'old quantum theory'. That title was soon shortened to the punchier 'quantum theory'. German physicist Max Planck led the charge with his discovery that energy was emitted or absorbed in finite units, or 'quanta'. Back in 1905, Einstein developed a quantum theory of light, showing that while light was previously thought to move in waves, it also exhibited particle-like properties, composed of quanta, what he now referred to as 'photons'. (In 1923 the theory was confirmed experimentally by the American physicist Arthur Compton.) A new model of atomic structure emerged in 1911 from the work of New Zealander physicist Ernest Rutherford, working at Cambridge, this model expanded in 1913 by the Dane Niels Bohr and shortly after by the German Arnold Sommerfeld. The Rutherford–Bohr–Sommerfeld model of atomic structure showed the atom not as a solid entity – contra J.J. Thomson's 'plum pudding' model (Thomson saw the newly discovered, negatively charged electrons embedded in a positively charged atomic mass like plums in a pudding) – but rather a central nucleus consisting of protons (positive) and neutrons (neutral), around which negatively charged electrons orbited, like planets circling a distant sun. This analogy is now obsolete, but it more accurately represented the energy state of the atom. Quantum theory then described how the electrons in atoms exist in discrete energy levels, or quantized states, rather than continuous orbits. The electrons can transition between these energy levels by absorbing or emitting specific amounts of energy (the quanta).

Quantum theory was a radical revisioning of fundamental physics, significantly modifying Sir Isaac Newton's classical mechanics and challenging textbook electromagnetic theory. But quantum theory produced as many problems as solutions, so triggered a vast intellectual and international arms race to go deeper into the behaviours of subatomic particles, and the associated mathematics.

The French physicist Louis de Broglie took the next great leap forward in quantum theory in 1924 with the concept of 'wave-particle duality', positing that electrons exhibit both wave-like and particle-like properties; the same characteristic could be applied to matter itself. The theory had a seismic impact upon theoretical physics, leading to the development of quantum mechanics in the mid-1920s, which explored wave-particle duality in depth. European physicists such as Werner Heisenberg, Pascual Jordan, Max Born and Wolfgang Paul in turn developed 'matrix mechanics' and provided a radical new insight into atomic properties and subatomic behaviours. This approach was complemented and later challenged by Erwin Schrödinger's alternative 'wave mechanics' model in 1926. Quantum theory led to quantum mechanics, which focused on the mathematical description of subatomic particles. Although much of the new science was perfectly impenetrable to outsiders, quantum theory was steadily remodelling humanity's understanding of the universe and the 'reality' that surrounds us. It was an arena for brilliant, youthful minds.

Oppenheimer's post-Harvard academic trajectory was essentially an effort to merge into the flow of quantum mechanics, while at the same time attempting to exorcize the demons of insecurity. His effort to do so would, for a time, be both messy and disastrous.

As his Harvard graduation loomed, Oppenheimer identified graduate study at Cambridge University as the next desirable step. The key to this transition was Professor Percy W. Bridgman. Oppenheimer had taken Bridgman's course in advanced thermodynamics, which proved to be one of the few Harvard courses Oppenheimer held in truly high regard. With Bridgman's advocacy, Oppenheimer hoped that Cambridge would open its doors to him. But the bar to entering Cambridge to study physics was set formidably high. Specifically, Oppenheimer wanted to join Rutherford's team working on cutting-edge atomic physics. Rutherford (officially Sir Ernest Rutherford, following his knighthood in 1908), was now director at the world-leading Cavendish Laboratory, and a Zeus-like figure among the pantheon of contemporary physicists. As well as a new atomic model, Rutherford had also classified three types of radiation (alpha, beta and gamma) and, in 1919, had artificially created a nuclear reaction in a stable element. If Oppenheimer would learn from anyone, it would be Rutherford.

Bridgman supported Oppenheimer's application to Cambridge, sending his endorsement directly to Rutherford. What he wrote, however, was no mere puff piece. The letter gives us significant insights into Oppenheimer's strengths and weaknesses as a young scientist seeking to find his metier. Bridgman emphasized the extraordinary nature of Oppenheimer's mind and memory, but also was honest about Oppenheimer's struggle when the theory went practical:

His problems have in many cases shown a high degree of originality in treatment and much mathematical power. His weakness is on the experimental side. His type of mind is analytical, rather than physical, and he is not at home in the manipulations of the laboratory [...] It appears to me that it is a bit of a gamble as to whether Oppenheimer will ever make any real contributions of an important character, but it he does make good at all, I believe that he will be a very unusual success, and if you are in a position to take a small gamble without too much trouble, I think you will seldom find a more interesting betting proposition.[22]

Bridgman describes a young man whose potential is formidable, but whose ability to fulfil that potential is far from assured. For Rutherford, Bridgman offers Oppenheimer as an audacious bet. We should note, also, that Bridgman pointed out Oppenheimer's Jewishness, but reassures Rutherford that he was 'entirely without the usual qualifications of his race' – we are left to queasy speculations about what he meant.

In a formal application letter to R.E. Priestley, the registrar at Christ's College, Oppenheimer defined more clearly his aspirations for study at Cambridge.

He outlined his vision of future academic progress at Cambridge, explaining that at the end of three years of study he hoped to graduate with a Doctorate of Philosophy. In preparation for his studies, he would 'like to continue reading in Physics, in Analysis, and in Physical Chemistry', but he also expressed how keen he was to find and pursue a research challenge in physics, clearly wanting to make his mark in a significant contemporary domain. Here Oppenheimer spelled out his current field of interest, namely the 'theory of electronic conduction'. From a specifically theoretical position, he wanted to explore 'the laws of force to which the motions of electrons are subject' and receive 'critical advice' on the direction and position. He also wanted support with engaging in further experimental work, perhaps sensing – and here we note Bridgman's concerns – that this side of his scientific ability was his weakest.[23]

Despite, or perhaps because of, Bridgman's letter, Oppenheimer did not secure his desired place on Rutherford's team. He was, however, accepted into Christ's College to study physics. His supervisor would be Professor J.J. Thomson, the Nobel Laureate in Physics who had discovered the electron, the first subatomic particle to be identified and named. Thomson was a towering figure, certainly, but by the mid-1920s he had a slight aura of being yesterday's man; Rutherford, one of his former students, was now at the tip of the spear. Still, Oppenheimer was accepted into Cambridge in one of the world's most prestigious research hubs for physics.

His next step confirmed, his studies at Harvard completed, Oppenheimer took a further break in New Mexico, this time travelling with Horgan. Refreshed from his trip, he arrived in Cambridge on 16 September 1925. He immediately met up with Fergusson and they embarked on a short walking holiday around Cornwall before their studies began.

Oppenheimer was in Cambridge, where he had wanted to go. He was studying physics at an advanced level, which is what he wanted to do. But he was about to descend into one of the most unhappy periods of his life, punctuated with some genuinely disconcerting episodes of mental fracture. The root causes of his troubles were deep, multiple and sinewy. First, he was insecure about his place at the University of Cambridge and within Cambridge society. For a young Jewish-American, Cambridge could appear impossibly other, full of polished, confident beings accustomed to breathing the crystalline air of high status. Fergusson was also an American, but Oppenheimer clearly saw him as effortlessly superior, producing a tension that would result in near-fatal consequences.

Cambridge was also the first educational experience of Oppenheimer's life in which he struggled to keep up with his peers. As Bridgman had identified, Oppenheimer seemed to have an inherent clumsiness in experimental physics. At Cambridge, Oppenheimer found himself surrounded by young scientists whose stellar brains were often boosted by high levels of amateur practical skills, from welding to carpentry. In this environment, Oppenheimer did not stand out as particularly exceptional, probably the first time in his life he had experienced this situation. Furthermore, Cambridge exposed an intellectual problem – Oppenheimer could be sloppy with his mathematics, an issue that would occasionally blight his research work well beyond the Cambridge years.

On the periphery of the social and academic elite, Oppenheimer felt he was pressing his nose on the glass from the outside, with the truly exciting work going on inside. In a letter to Fergusson on 15 November 1925, he explained that 'there is, really, a new generation [of physicists], and for the first time they have got people here who do both theory and experiment'.[24] Compounding his sense of difference, possibly of inferiority, was the simple fact that he was lonely. In the same letter, he spoke to Fergusson of 'some terrible complications with Fred [Bernheim]' – the 'awful evening' in which Bernheim explained their effective separation as friends – and that he hadn't see him since.

The cumulative effects of his insecurities coalesced into the perfect psychological storm. Fergusson himself recorded Oppenheimer's mental unravelling in a document he composed in February 1926, entitled 'Account of the Adventures of Robert Oppenheimer in Europe'. The exact purpose of the document is unclear, but it is apparent that Fergusson saw an opportunity for psychoanalysis in his troubled, fascinating friend. Fergusson noted that on arrival in Cambridge Oppenheimer seemed to be in robust mental health, but that within months he had descended into a 'first class case of depression'.[25] His parents, informed by letters, grew increasingly concerned for their son's well-being, so crossed the Atlantic to see him. Oppenheimer took the train from Cambridge to meet them on their arrival at Southampton.

On the train, Fergusson recounts, Oppenheimer was treated to the extraordinary spectacle of a man and woman having unrestrained sex right in front of him in a third-class carriage. While they were doing so, Oppenheimer stoically pretended to consult a tome on thermodynamics. The relationship between the amorous pair was evidently not profound, as the man left shortly after. Clearly in a state of sexual confusion, Oppenheimer then launched forward and kissed the woman, following up on his boldness by dropping to his knees in tears and begging forgiveness. He could have left it there, but at Southampton station Oppenheimer evidently decided that he needed to take action. He deliberately dropped his heavy suitcase from an elevated position on a flight of stairs, attempting to hit the woman below him. Fortunately it missed.

His parents arrived straight into what was evidently a severe mental health crisis for their son, and they may well have compounded it. They had in tow Oppenheimer's childhood friend Inez Pollak, who was clearly bemused at being there. Fergusson believed that Julius and Ella wanted to arrange a romance between Robert and Inez, to lift his mood. It didn't end well. Back in Cambridge, the parental efforts led to nothing but another disastrous sexual encounter for Oppenheimer, with both he and Inez reduced to sobbing in his room while Ella obsessively banged on the door asking to be let in. Ella, judiciously, left soon after.

Oppenheimer's sexual chaos was not even the summit of his strange behaviour. To help with his experimental work, Oppenheimer was assigned a tutor, Professor Patrick Blackett. Blackett was not only a superb physicist – in 1948 he would win the Nobel Prize in Physics for his 'development of the Wilson cloud chamber method, and his discoveries therewith in the fields of nuclear physics and cosmic radiation'[26] – he was also something of an Apollonian figure on campus, described by the future literary critic Ivor Richards (at that time a college friend of Blackett) as 'a young Oedipus. Tall, slim, beautifully balanced and always looking better dressed than anyone.'[27] Blackett compounded his charms by having a beautiful wife and by being a genuine, likeable person, his left-wing leanings giving him an additional allure on campus. Oppenheimer seems to have developed an intolerable obsession with Blackett, largely through making crippling comparisons between himself and the graceful tutor, not least because Blackett also had the nimble and confident hands to be a brilliant experimental physicist. Matters came to a head when Oppenheimer apparently laced an apple with toxic chemicals – possibly cyanide – and left it on Blackett's desk as a potentially lethal gift. Thankfully, the apple remained uneaten, but Oppenheimer's mad act was discovered. Julius Oppenheimer reasoned with Cambridge not to expel his son on account of his mental illness; impressively, Cambridge agreed, placing Oppenheimer on probation on the condition that he attended psychiatric therapy.[28]

Unfortunately, Oppenheimer's murderous impulses were not yet fully exorcized. After his first term, he went to France with his parents, meeting Fergusson in Paris. He cut a strange, staring, disturbed figure. In one incident, he locked his mother in her hotel room. When she was finally released, she took her confounding son to see a French psychiatrist, who diagnosed Oppenheimer with 'sexual frustration', which apparently could be cured by a prescribed trip to a prostitute.[29] But much worse was still to come. Oppenheimer went to visit Fergusson in his Parisian hotel room. Once in the room, he told Fergusson that he was now engaged to a woman called Frances Keeley (she was indeed his girlfriend at this time). Then, when Fergusson's back was turned, Oppenheimer suddenly leapt on his friend and attempted to strangle him with a luggage strap. Fergusson, by far the stronger of the two, managed to break free, after which Oppenheimer fell to the floor sobbing. Only later, back in Cambridge, did Oppenheimer send a prostrate letter apologizing to Fergusson, expressing the 'shame I feel for my inadequacy to you'.[30] Later in March 1926, he wrote again to say that he had now reached a different place, stating: 'My regret at not having strangled you is now intellectual rather than emotional,'[31] and saying that it was now safe for Fergusson to visit him. Given that the two men would have a lifelong friendship, clearly Fergusson had a forgiving or at least understanding personality.

Oppenheimer's time at Cambridge was not, it should be said, a total disaster, however much it teetered on the brink of that outcome. He managed to put down some solid intellectual foundations and make some important professional connections, both of which would have an important impact on his future. Most significant was that while at Cambridge Oppenheimer published his first two papers. The first was presented in the famous *Proceedings* of the Cambridge Philosophical Society in July 1926. It was entitled 'On the Quantum Theory of Vibration-Rotation Bands'. This paper applied quantum mechanics to diatomic molecules (molecules that consisted of two atoms), the introduction declaring that 'The dynamical problem of the "diatomic molecule" is solved on the new mechanics.' The paper was a decent start to his academic publishing career, migrating Paul Dirac's mathematic formulations of quantum mechanics into molecular physics, but it contained some embarrassing mathematical errors. These slips would not be his last in published works. Nevertheless, the paper brought him to the attention of some influential theoretical physicists, not least the Austrian theoretical physicist Paul Ehrenfest of the University of Leiden, Germany. Oppenheimer spent a fruitful week in Leiden meeting Ehrenfest and his assistants, laying the groundwork for a reconnection in the near future.

The second paper Oppenheimer produced was more significant to his reputation-building. It was entitled 'On the Quantum Theory of the Problem of the Two Bodies'. Classically, the two-body problem referred to the challenge of predicting the motion of two particles interacting with one another only via the energy of each other. In his paper, Oppenheimer took quantum mechanics and applied it to this problem with ambition, setting his ideas among those of some of the leading physicists of the day:

The problem of the two bodies has been treated on the new mechanics by Dirac, Pauli, and Schrödinger, who have independently derived the Balmer terms. The present paper is an attempt at a more complete solution. In particular, formulae are derived for the line intensities of the hydrogen spectrum, for the photoelectric effect and its inverse, and for the continuous absorption spectrum in the ultraviolet and in the X-ray regions. Also the probabilities of transition, deflection and capture are computed for the collision of an electron and an ion. Numerical values are only obtained, however, for the simplest line intensities. It is hoped to treat the problem in greater detail.[32]

This second paper was genuinely impactful within contemporary and future physics, aided by the fact that Oppenheimer took extra care to ensure that all the mathematical work was correct. While conducting his research, he also had the opportunity to meet with the Nobel Prize-winning physicist Niels Bohr, who was visiting Cambridge and who tightened Oppenheimer's interest in pursuing theoretical rather than experimental physics. More important, Oppenheimer also came to the attention of Max Born from the University of Göttingen in Germany.

Born had transformed the direction of quantum mechanics in 1926 with his paper 'On the Quantum mechanics of collision processes'. Born had demonstrated that in quantum mechanics the movement of particles does not follow a strict and predictable pattern of cause and effect, but instead follows non-deterministic probability patterns. Under this theory, we can only state the probability of the position of an electron; in reality, any position is possible. It was an important paper for physics, but also for Oppenheimer, in that Born acknowledged the contribution of Oppenheimer's second paper to his new theory. Born also had Oppenheimer translate a subsequent major paper for publication in *Nature*.

Oppenheimer was now getting known. Despite all the chaos of the year in Cambridge, his mind was also finding some clarity. He would put aside experimental physics and instead focus on his true passion, theoretical physics. With this in mind, he applied to spend his following year of study working with Born in Göttingen, a request that was approved. It would constitute one of the most significant decisions of his early career.

GÖTTINGEN

Oppenheimer's first year in Cambridge was a deeply unhappy period for the young physicist. Oppenheimer still carried some of his demons to Göttingen, arriving there in the late summer of 1926. Over the course of the subsequent year in Germany, he would have flashes of mental disorder, depression, self-loathing and panic. But overall, Göttingen reshaped him. He would emerge more confident, self-assured, stable, popular and, above all, *recognized*. The brilliance of his mind, now exposed from beneath the veil of mental illness, shone like the stars he would spend much of his future researching, visible to all those around him.

It is important to understand that at this time in the history of science, Germany was *the* centre of the new physics. Cambridge might have been the home of experimental physics, but it was at places such as Göttingen that the truly pioneering theoretical work on quantum theory was being done. At Göttingen, therefore, Oppenheimer stepped into the deep and fast-flowing waters of cutting-edge theoretical physics. He now had the opportunity to mix, discuss and argue with the leading minds in the field. This elite group not only included Born, but also the upcoming American physicists Karl Taylor Compton and Edward Condon, the Dutch-American theoretical physicists George Eugene Uhlenbeck and Samuel Goudsmit, the future Nobel Laureate Maria Göppert (later Maria Goeppert Mayer), future Nobel Prize winners Paul Dirac and James Franck, and the brilliant Hungarian-American mathematician John von Neumann – a list that is far from exhaustive.

One factor above all made this crowded field of luminaries distinct – its leaning towards youth. Many of these individuals were, at the time, in their 20s, and often at the lower end of this age bracket. The reverence towards ageing figures such as Albert Einstein, who

With his back to the camera, fifth from right, Oppenheimer stands with colleagues and their wives in this photograph from Göttingen, 1927.

became critically suspicious of developments in quantum theory, was beginning to wane, especially once Einstein broke publicly with Werner Heisenberg's theories of indeterminacy. (It is this clash that elicited Einstein's famous quotation, 'God does not play dice.') Austrian physicist Wolfgang Pauli labelled quantum mechanics as *Knabenphysik* – 'boys' physics' – such was its capture by young minds.

At Göttingen, Oppenheimer became a leading member of the *Knabenphysik*. He also felt at home in European culture (he spoke German fluently, and soon picked up Italian and Dutch at the same level), although he also observed the caustic politics entrenched in Weimar Germany, auguring darker times for Europe. Such was his immersion in European physics that he expressed some generalized disdain for American physicists, on account of their age profile and intellectual constraints. In a letter to Fergusson on 14 November 1926 he explains: 'There are about 20 American physicists & such here. Most of them are over thirty, Professors at Princeton or California or some such place, married, respectable. They are mostly pretty good at physics, but completely uneducated & unspoiled. They envy the Germans their intellectual adroitness & organization, & want physics to come to America.'[33]

The arrogance others often noted in Oppenheimer is apparent here. Indeed, Göttingen did absolutely nothing to teach Oppenheimer humility; if anything, he retained his instinctive desire to outperform and reduce many of those around him, if he sensed weakness. A composite of feedback from those who knew Oppenheimer personally suggests a person who either sized up people he wished to emulate – to them he was giving, generous and attentive – and those he felt were beneath him. To the latter, he could be transparently disdainful.

The truth was, however, Oppenheimer could treat people high-handedly and get away with it largely because he *was* usually the most exceptional person in the room, at least intellectually. If he couldn't dominate the conversation in physics (which was rare), then he could draw out his encyclopaedic cultural knowledge to subdue and impress. He was capable of appalling condescension. One individual who saw this first hand was Condon. Although Condon was a highly capable physicist, of similar age to Oppenheimer, unlike his affluent associate Condon had a wife (Emilie) and an infant child, the young family struggling to survive on a small academic income. Oppenheimer on one occasion invited the Condons out for a walk. Emilie politely refused because of childcare responsibilities, to which Oppenheimer replied: 'All right, we'll leave you to your peasant duties.'[34]

Condon was far from the only person at Göttingen who came into contact with Oppenheimer's hauteur. It also extended into the academic setting. In seminars held by none other than Max Born, Oppenheimer would keep dismissively interrupting the presentation or discussion, declaring that everything being said was wrong, even striding up to the blackboard to demonstrate the correct approach. Oppenheimer's walked a fine line between confidence and intimidation; Born himself later admitted to feeling undermined and dominated by Oppenheimer, aware of the sometimes cruel brilliance of this young student.

Others were less cowed. One undergraduate student, Maria Göppert (who would go on to become the second woman in history to win the Nobel Prize in Physics), had enough of Oppenheimer's continual interruptions. She wrote a letter to Born stating that if Oppenheimer wasn't brought under control then the students would start boycotting the seminars. Born had to act but was nervous about a direct confrontation with Oppenheimer. Instead, he invited Oppenheimer round to his home and left Göppert's letter lying on his desk. He then contrived to leave Oppenheimer alone in the room. Oppenheimer evidently read the letter, as he returned to the seminars a quieter man.

The problem for many who ran up against Oppenheimer is that he was verbally and conceptually outperforming most of those around him. One student commented that 'I felt as if he were an inhabitant of Olympus who had strayed among humans and was doing his best to appear human.'[35] Born promoted Oppenheimer's exceptionalism, explaining to an enquiring Rockefeller Foundation that as a young American physicist Oppenheimer 'rises above the average'.

Oppenheimer's intellect soared, certainly, but this did not mean he was a natural communicator, certainly not an educator in the Feynman tradition. In both speech and writing, he was notoriously complex, often pushing beyond the comprehension of all but the most brilliant interlocutors. Nevertheless, at Göttingen he published seven papers, clearly finding his rhythm and market. His published works entered a crowded, brilliant field, sitting alongside ground-breaking works by the likes of Paul Dirac, responsible for critical shifts in theoretical physics such as transformation theory and quantum electrodynamics, and Heisenberg, who in 1927 established a new framework for quantum theory with his uncertainty principle.

But Oppenheimer was now becoming a leading figure in new-generation physics. Two of his papers deserve special mention. The first, entitled 'Zur Quantentheorie kontinuierlicher Spektren' ('On the Quantum Theory of Continuous Spectra'), was the basis of his PhD thesis. This paper applied quantum mechanics to calculating the absorption of light by hydrogen. The technique outlined had – and has to this day – significant applications for understanding the internal processes of stars.

The second paper of note established what is today known as the 'Born–Oppenheimer approximation', a method for calculating the energy states of molecules using quantum mechanics. This paper addressed one of the most formidable challenges in contemporary physics. Just calculating the energy states of a single hydrogen atom – the simplest atomic structure, consisting of one proton and one electron – was in physics a task of daunting effort. Calculating the energy states of a *molecule*, which consists of two or more atoms, almost all of greater complexity than hydrogen, presented what appeared to be a prohibitively massive expansion of the mathematical problem. Oppenheimer moved towards solving it first by imagining nuclei as stationary, rather than incorporating their vibrational energies, then calculating the energies of the electrons before factoring nucleic vibrations back in, then deriving the rotational energy of the molecule. The output from this strategy was not exact – hence the word 'approximation' – but it was accurate enough to give physicists a practical tool to calculate molecular energy. It also helped lay the foundations of a new field of study: quantum chemistry.

The production of this paper was not a smooth collaboration between Oppenheimer and his supervisor, Born. Despite the name 'Born–Oppenheimer approximation', it is generally taken for granted that the majority of the work was Oppenheimer's effort. Oppenheimer's first iteration of the paper was only five dense pages. Born felt that this fell short of what was required, and so compelled a major expansion, under his direction and against Oppenheimer's will. Nevertheless, the final output was well received by its audience upon publication. Indeed, Oppenheimer secured his doctorate on its basis.

Of all the people at Göttingen, Born seems to have been the most bruised by his prolonged struggles with Oppenheimer, or rather his sense that Oppenheimer's mind was greater than his own. He confessed to Paul Ehrenfest that 'My soul was nearly destroyed by that man.'[36] But with his doctorate complete, Oppenheimer left Göttingen in September 1927.

Göttingen was crucial for Oppenheimer. His success there galvanized his confidence and placed him visibly on the top table of international theoretical physicists. We should also point out that while the number of true, intimate friends Oppenheimer made at Göttingen were few, he was nevertheless accepted into the culture and the community of the university. He also had his first relatively successful romance, dating doctoral student Charlotte Riefenstahl. They separated amicably when he left Göttingen, although she would reappear briefly in his life (see opposite). But Göttingen was a place where, among academics, brilliance was of greater importance than most other qualities, and Oppenheimer had it in spades. Furthermore, he had expanded his network of connections into the new generation of physicists. Many of those he met at Göttingen would later gather at Los Alamos to pursue work of a very different nature.

POSTDOCTORAL STUDIES

The world of physics was taking notice of J. Robert Oppenheimer. During the later months of his study at Göttingen he began receiving many unprompted offers for both jobs and further work opportunities. They came from revered universities – Berlin, Harvard, Leipzig, Princeton, Columbia, Chicago, Sorbonne. But the offer that attracted his attention most was that of a postdoctoral fellowship from the US National Research Council (NRC). Oppenheimer had enjoyed Göttingen, but decided not to stay in Europe, yearning to get back to the energy of New York, the closeness to family (especially his brother Frank) and the dusty freedom of New Mexico. Thus he accepted NRC fellowships to study at both Harvard and the California Institute of Technology (Caltech).

On his initial return to New York, some parts of Europe followed him. Charlotte Riefenstahl, temporarily in the company of none other than Goudsmit and Uhlenbeck, had come to New York to take up a teaching position at Vassar College, Poughkeepsie. Together the four formed a reunited pack, Oppenheimer relishing the opportunity to show them the big city. Romance between Oppenheimer and Riefenstahl flowered briefly, but Oppenheimer's challenging nature appears to have made Charlotte cautious, and they soon drifted apart permanently. Of note is that she later married Friedrich 'Fritz' Houtermans, a German atomic/nuclear physicist whom Oppenheimer had got to know at Göttingen. Houtermans' experience during the war years was tumultuous to say the least, but he eventually worked, reluctantly, on the German atomic bomb project.

The failed relationship with Charlotte, one in a growing line of dysfunctional attempts at romance, might have skewed Oppenheimer's attitude towards women. In a letter to his brother Frank, who was also experiencing some conflicted feelings about the opposite sex, Oppenheimer gave blunt advice that somehow managed to raise more questions than solutions: 'Don't worry about girls, and don't make love to girls, unless you have to: DON'T DO IT AS A DUTY.'[37] The caution not to make love 'unless you have to' begs the question about what grinding emergency might necessitate sex as duty rather than pleasure. It likely indicates that Oppenheimer was, at this stage of his life, still inexperienced with relationships.

Following his time in New York, Oppenheimer then headed for Massachusetts to begin his academic term at Harvard. He soon published two more scientific papers, but he also found time to indulge his love of poetry. One of his poems, entitled 'Crossing', was actually published in the June 1928 issue of the Harvard-produced miscellany *Hound and Horn*. It is worth reproducing in its entirety, as it enables us to gaze upon an emotional landscape that was clearly important to Oppenheimer:

Crossing
It was evening when we came to the river
with a low moon over the desert
that we had lost in the mountains, forgotten,
what with the cold and the sweating
and the ranges barring the sky.
And when we found it again,
in the dry hills down by the river,
half withered, we had
the hot winds against us.

There were two palms by the landing;
the yuccas were flowering; there was
a light on the far shore, and tamarisks.

We waited a long time, in silence.

Then we heard the oars creaking

and afterwards, I remember,

the boatman called to us.

We did not look back at the mountains.[38]

The poem is mature and well-composed. Oppenheimer clearly had a talent for expression, and his ability with phrase and imagery would be a key factor in his later public profile. But the work also shows the elegiac bond between Oppenheimer and New Mexico, his intimacy with its terrain, flora and fauna, weather, heights. We can debate the implication of the final encounter with the boatman, a figure of death and loss; perhaps New Mexico is both homecoming and final destination.

After five months at Harvard, Oppenheimer moved to the southwest to Caltech, continuing his postdoctoral fellowship. He was receiving a steady inflow of job offers, and as time passed it was clear that he would have to make a firm decision about his next step. The final choice was something of a hybrid. He negotiated professorships at both Caltech and at the University of California, Berkeley. Berkeley in particular was an exciting prospect for Oppenheimer – it had no theoretical physics department and thus gave him the opportunity to build an institution from scratch. This could be the American Göttingen. Notably, Oppenheimer turned down earnest job offers from Harvard, despite the prestige a post at that university might bring. However, he also negotiated a year's hiatus between completing his term at Caltech and commencing his professorships. Funded again by the NRC, he would spend the intervening time back in Europe, conducting postdoctoral research among some of the continent's finest minds working on quantum mechanics.

The fellowship at Caltech drew to a close in July 1928. Before heading out to Europe once again, Oppenheimer made a trip to Ann Arbor, where a pleasant time was had with Goudsmit and Uhlenbeck (who were still in the country) and while attending a summer school in theoretical physics. Oppenheimer also informed the International Education Board at the Rockefeller Foundation (which had oversight of the NRC fellowship) that he was suffering from tuberculosis and on medical advice would have to postpone the start of his European fellowship. Although Oppenheimer did display a persistent bad cough, and could have rather frail health, there is some doubt about whether he actually had TB or not. A subsequent NRC-mandated medical found no evidence of the condition, plus Oppenheimer was certainly well enough to take a restorative trip to New Mexico to meet with his beloved brother Frank, who was also at this stage gravitating towards a career in physics. They met once again with Katherine Chaves Page, who took the brothers out to see a beguiling log cabin in the mountains. The cabin, and 154 acres of adjacent land, were available to rent, and Robert convinced his father to move on this opportunity. They would call the cabin *Perro Caliente*, the Spanish translation of the English exclamation 'Hog Dog!', which Oppenheimer uttered involuntarily when shown the cabin.

Finally, Oppenheimer's delayed European adventure began in November 1927. The first port of call was the University of Leiden in the Netherlands, where he began a productive period of research under Ehrenfest. Like the relationship between Born and Oppenheimer, that between Oppenheimer and Ehrenfest was held under tension. Ehrenfest was less deferential towards Oppenheimer than

Born, however, regarding Oppenheimer as undoubtedly brilliant but also lacking discipline and control, compounded by his tendency towards arrogance. Oppenheimer conversely found Ehrenfest a gloomy and introspective figure. Ehrenfest was undoubtedly mired in depression, struggling to cope with the pressures of his career, but also those of coping with a young son with Down's Syndrome. In a tragic future, on 25 September 1933 Ehrenfest killed his son before committing suicide.

But for Oppenheimer, his time at Leiden was stimulating and enjoyable. He loved the culture of the Netherlands. Naturally, he taught himself Dutch to such a state of fluency that he was able to lecture in it. He also acquired a nickname from the Dutch students

Outside Heike Kamerlingh Onnes's laboratory in Leiden, Netherlands, July 1927. Oppenheimer is in the second row from the back, second from left.

– *Opje*. This one would stick beyond Europe, being transplanted back to the USA for his close friends as 'Oppie'.

From Leiden, Oppenheimer's next research destination was Zurich, Switzerland. There he worked with Wolfgang Pauli, the ground-breaking theorist defining the new field of quantum electrodynamics, which fused the principles of quantum mechanics with the theory of electromagnetism, explaining phenomena such as how electrons and photons interact. Oppenheimer travelled to Zurich via Leipzig, taking the opportunity to hear the great Werner Heisenberg give a presentation on ferromagnetism.

At Zurich, Oppenheimer and Pauli developed solid mutual respect. Pauli, brilliant and tough in equal measure, was not in the slightest intimidated by Oppenheimer's precocity. He appreciated Oppenheimer's leaps of insight, but was also, like Ehrenfest, critical of his failings when it came to detail and discipline. It was a useful relationship for Oppenheimer, tightening up his thinking. He also furthered his personal and professional network at Zurich. He met another high-flying Jewish-American physics student, Isidor I. Rabi. In contrast with Oppenheimer's affluence, Rabi grew up in poverty and hardship, but they forged a lasting friendship, helped by the fact that both men were interested in culture and ideas outside science. Oppenheimer also met and befriended Swiss-American physicist Felix Bloch, another future Nobel Prize winner. Bloch particularly remembered, with a trace of irritation, how Oppenheimer would gush with enthusiasm over the USA, his Zurich apartment heavily decorated with furnishings and artefacts from back home.

Oppenheimer's second academic period in Europe furthered his intellectual accomplishments. In total, Oppenheimer published

16 papers between 1926 and 1929, a formidable output. Oppenheimer biographers Kai Bird and Martin J. Sherwin, authors of the seminal *American Prometheus*, summarized the breadth of his achievements in physics during this time:

> He was the first physicist to master the nature of continuum wave functions. His most original contribution, in the opinion of the physicist Robert Serber, was his theory of field emission, an approach that permitted him to study the emission of electrons from metals, induced by a very strong field. In these early years he was able to achieve breakthroughs in the calculation of the absorption coefficient of X rays and the inelastic scattering of electrons.[39]

In any other academic, this work would be a purely intellectual landmark, an achievement within the specific and often cloistered domain of academia. But for Oppenheimer, each paper, each theory conceived, was a step towards his landmark work between 1942 and 1945.

Now it was time to go home.

CHAPTER 3

LEANING TO THE LEFT

The period from 1929 to 1941 transformed America. It began catastrophically, with the Wall Street Crash of September and October 1929, the catalyst for the devastating Great Depression that swept the globe. Although this hung over the USA for the rest of the decade, the country began its spectacular climb out of financial hardship in 1933, destined to become our planet's economic colossus. In December 1941, the USA entered the world war that had flared in Europe in September 1939, at first as a relative military minnow, but eventually the superpower which would, with the Soviet Union, essentially win the war. This was the age that built modern America.

Apparently, the Oppenheimer family survived the turmoil of the depression with little disturbance to Robert. According to biographer Ray Monk, Oppenheimer was later told about the Wall Street Crash by physicist Ernest Lawrence many months after it had occurred; such was his disconnect from current affairs that he was blissfully unaware that it had happened. But while Oppenheimer was detached from his nation's struggles during the pre-war years, his personal and professional transformation would be great. During this decade he took a leading role in creating modern American theoretical physics, with cutting-edge research that no longer lagged behind that of Europe. He did not, for all his brilliance, do this single-handedly – there were many other minds, some arguably superior to Oppenheimer, who also turned on the power to

American physics. But Oppenheimer's contribution was seminal, and it put him on the path to Los Alamos. Furthermore, the pre-war years invoked in Oppenheimer a political reawakening. That, as we shall see, would bring as much trouble as enlightenment.

CALTECH AND BERKELEY

Oppenheimer began his professional academic career alternating between Caltech in Pasadena and the University of California, Berkeley, teaching one semester at each. Both institutions already had well-established physics departments. Caltech had founded its Division of Physics in 1917. Some of its subsequent leading lights

Oppenheimer (left) and Ernest Orlando Lawrence (right) became close friends during their time at Berkeley. This rather eccentric picture was taken at Perro Caliente in the early 1930s. Lawrence would win the Nobel Prize in 1939 for his invention of the cyclotron.

include Richard C. Tolman, who was already Oppenheimer's friend when he arrived in 1929, and Robert Andrews Millikan, who had received the Nobel Prize in Physics for his work on the magnitude of an electron's charge and was chairman of the Executive Council of Caltech, the institution's governing body. (Millikan would go on to have a far more fractious relationship with Oppenheimer.) Also working at Caltech on Oppenheimer's arrival was the Danish-American physicist Charles Lauritsen; both Tolman and Lauritsen would later work within the Manhattan Project.

Berkeley had a somewhat weaker tradition in physics, and especially in theoretical physics, but that is not to say that Oppenheimer was working with a blank slate. The likes of Gilbert N. Lewis, Raymond T. Birge and Leonard Loeb had already conducted important physics research at Berkeley. Furthermore, and with much significance for the future, when Oppenheimer arrived the nuclear physicist Ernest Orlando Lawrence was already there, developing the world's first 'cyclotron' – a particle accelerator – which would be up and running by 1931 and for which Lawrence would receive the Nobel Prize in 1939.

Yet at both Caltech and Berkeley, particularly the latter, it was Oppenheimer who had the transformative effect. In the field of theoretical physics, and especially in the new quantum domain, he brought energy, innovation and ideas every bit equal to what was happening in Europe. His astounding mind, his unique style of teaching and his absorbed passion for the subject all meant that before long Berkeley was a globally respected centre for physics.

But when Oppenheimer began his professorships he was by no means a natural-born teacher. Indeed, his early teaching style tended to confound more than clarify. Taking his own later self-analysis, and the views of those who witnessed his performance in seminar rooms and lecture theatres, the problem seemed to be rooted in the fact that Oppenheimer did not really see himself as there to teach. Rather, his mission was to interrogate the topic of theoretical physics and pursue it fearlessly, without restraint. The problem was that Oppenheimer's brain worked on a superior level, and he expected others to have the same mental speed and reach. He was teaching bright students – all in his classes were either graduate students or postdoctoral researchers – but most felt they were just running behind Oppenheimer's accelerating car as it sped into the distance. During one of his first lectures, Tolman attended at the back of the room. At the end, the students filed out silently. Tolman approached Oppenheimer and gave and then retracted a compliment: 'Well, Robert, that was beautiful but I didn't understand a damn word.'[40] The common takeaway from many of Oppenheimer's early lectures was sheer incomprehensibility.

Oppenheimer's expectations were simply too high. He assumed, for example, that students would be able to read difficult scientific papers in German, Dutch and other languages. Oppenheimer himself viewed the problem from an opposite direction, telling Birge 'I'm going so slowly that I'm not getting anywhere.'[41] Oppenheimer wanted to push theoretical physics to and over the horizon, and seemed to feel that the students were acting as an intellectual sea anchor, holding back progress.

Worse than Oppenheimer's lack of empathy as an instructor was his academic cruelty. In seminars, he would openly deride half-formed student theories, cutting the anxious speaker off mid-sentence if he saw a problem or platitude. He would unleash arcane cultural references that made the room feel uneducated.

He could also be bitingly sarcastic. On the plus side, he tended to be more generous in one-to-one settings, encouraging students to discuss their problems with him, and offering to work with them to find solutions.

Thankfully, as Oppenheimer bedded into the university system he gained enough self-awareness to reform his approach to teaching. His language became simpler and more direct, focusing on comprehension at the point of entry. There was less showboating and sarcasm. Oppenheimer never relaxed his vertiginously high standards – he demanded unremittingly high standards from his students – but he gained a greater insight into what it meant to be an educator as well as a physicist.

Once the penny dropped, Oppenheimer's lectures become compulsive viewing, renowned not only for their clarity of construction but also their beauty of expression. Oppenheimer's absorbed passion, his encyclopaedic knowledge, rubbed off on those who attended his presentations and discussions. Many students unnecessarily attended the same course two, three, even four times, the repeated visits prompted simply by the wish to hear Oppenheimer's mind in flight once again. He also conducted close, intense seminars, giving each student time to speak and receive feedback. Such was the affection and respect for 'Oppie' (as he was known at Berkeley) or 'Robert' (Caltech), that other professors noticed students unconsciously emulating his mannerisms – his peculiar gait, thoughtful pauses in his speech, face-rubbing gestures, even his chain-smoking and accompanying cough. Students came to adore Oppenheimer.

Oppenheimer's personal popularity among students, therefore, was in the ascendant. His dating life remained complicated, characterized generally by short-lived episodes. Some observed an attraction towards married women, Oppenheimer giving them his full attention, as well as gifts such as flowers and confectionery. The days of awkwardness were disappearing. Oppenheimer could be both flirtatious and charming, and had 'an eye for the women' according to student Helen Allison from Caltech. But what relationships he did have were often compromised by a distracted mind. On one occasion in February 1934, Oppenheimer took Melba Phillips, his first graduate student, for a romantic drive up into the hills above Berkeley. They parked up in a remote spot, but Oppenheimer then became internally absorbed in a physics problem and walked back to his accommodation in the Berkeley faculty club, lost in thought and forgetting both car and passenger. The distraught Phillips was later rescued by police, according to the subsequent story published in the *San Francisco Chronicle* on 14 February 1934.

Cars and girls were not a good mix for Oppenheimer. Another short-term girlfriend, Natalie Raymond, ended up unconscious when Oppenheimer crashed his car, in which she was a passenger, while he was attempting to race a fast-moving train. Oppenheimer initially thought that Raymond was dead, but thankfully she made a full recovery – Julius Oppenheimer compensated her with gifts of art.

Generally speaking, automobiles seemed to bring out the devil in both Robert and Frank. On one occasion, the brothers were sharing the drive between New Mexico and Pasadena in their newly purchased Chrysler Roadster. Frank lost control and slewed off-road into a ditch. The car rolled and in the tumble Robert ended up with a broken arm. The next day, the car was retrieved, but disaster struck again when Frank drove the car straight into a slab of desert rock. Both men were unhurt, but the car was stuck fast and they spent the night in the desert. Robert Oppenheimer was himself a gleefully fast and reckless driver. Apparently this was a source of some pride, as evidenced in a letter to Frank in October 1929: 'From time to time I take out the Chrysler, and scare one of my friends out of all sanity by wheeling corners at seventy. [...] I am and shall be a vile driver.'[42]

Documents and memories from the 1930s throw further light on Oppenheimer's personal quirks. For example, he ate incredibly sparingly, which explains the lean, wiry frame he maintained throughout his life. (He was also a chain-smoker, which naturally suppresses appetite.) The problem was that he expected those around him to have the same meagre appetites. Regular guests to his house soon learned to have some concealed back-up food to assuage their hunger. But Oppenheimer's culinary tastes also leaned towards the exotic and spicy, at least by 1930s American standards. Else Uhlenbeck, the wife of George, taught Oppenheimer how to cook the traditional Indonesian dish *nasi goreng*. Oppenheimer would pour much effort into this dish but was heavy-handed on the peppers and spices, creating a repast suited only to guests with powers of endurance. Secretly, it became known to his guests as 'nasty gory'. Oppenheimer was also fond of cooking egg dishes, adding Mexican chillies to create 'Eggs à la Oppie'.

While Oppenheimer's professional life became one of exponential success, his personal life took a major blow in the autumn of 1931. Ella Oppenheimer's health was at this time in freefall. She had contracted leukaemia in the early part of the decade. Oppenheimer made several vigilant trips to visit her, but on 6 October

1931 a blunt telegram arrived from his father: 'Mother critically ill. Not expected to live.'[43] According to an observer, Oppenheimer was stunned by the news, and rushed to New York. Ella Oppenheimer died on 17 October.

Oppenheimer's relationship with his mother was not straightforward, but Herbert Smith was 'sure that he just worshipped [her].'[44] Smith actually went to visit the Oppenheimer apartment in New York when Ella was dying. He found himself sitting with Robert in a room adjacent to Ella's. Oppenheimer was leafing briskly through a book and Smith remarked how wonderful it must be to be able to read and absorb information at Oppenheimer's speed, to which Oppenheimer replied with a telling non sequitur: 'I am the loneliest man in the world.'[45] In his 1974 interview, Smith observed that this quotation had been often repeated in subsequent biographies, as if it directly applied as a response to Ella's death. But Smith seems to suggest that the phrase can be read in a broader light – with his mother's death, Oppenheimer was acutely aware of the very small number of people who loved him unconditionally. Oppenheimer now transferred his filial concern to his elderly father.

Oppenheimer was fundamentally a scientist and rationalist, but it is worth exploring his deeper spirituality and how that contextualized his life's vagaries and losses. His birth religion, Judaism, seems to have offered him little in the way of a spiritual crutch; Oppenheimer's cultural secularization was too deeply baked for him to return to his ancestral faith. Instead, his bespoke spirituality seemed to be composed of three influences – Hinduism, literature and psychoanalysis.

Oppenheimer's interest in Hinduism was sparked during his years at Harvard, when he read the core texts of the religion in

English translation. Clearly that was not enough. From 1933, Oppenheimer began to take lessons in Sanskrit from Arthur Ryder, the professor of Sanskrit language at Berkeley, and someone whom Oppenheimer came to respect greatly as a humane, modern teacher. True to form, Oppenheimer soaked up the ancient language at speed and was soon reading the seminal works of Hinduism in their original voice – the *Bhagavad Gita*, the *Meghaduta*, the *Rigveda*, the *Satakatraya*, the *Upanishads*. The *Bhagavad Gita*, that epic dialogue between Arjuna and Krishna within the *Mahabharata*, was especially compelling to Oppenheimer, who later referred to it as 'the most beautiful philosophical song existing in any known tongue'. This work, and Hinduism in general, punctuated Oppenheimer's moral discourse, most famously at the moment of the first atomic bomb test in July 1945, but also through his personal and public struggles over the Hiroshima and Nagasaki bombings and the subsequent atomic arms race. Less reverentially, he also gave one of his cars the nickname 'Garuda', a Hindu deity.

Isidor Rabi, a close judge of Oppenheimer's character, felt that Hinduism was for Oppenheimer part of a boundless vision of intellect and human capacity:

Oppenheimer was overeducated in those fields which lie outside the scientific tradition, such as his interest in religion, in the Hindu religion in particular, which resulted in a feeling for the mystery of the universe that surrounded him almost like a fog. He saw physics clearly, looking toward what had already been done, but at the border he tended to feel there was much more of the mysterious and novel than there actually was ... [he turned] away from the hard, crude methods of theoretical physics into a mystical realm of broad intuition.... In Oppenheimer the element of earthiness was feeble. Yet it was essentially this spiritual quality, this refinement as expressed in speech and manner, that was the basis of his charisma. He never expressed himself completely. He always left a feeling that there were depths of sensibility and insight not yet revealed. These may be the qualities of the born leader who seems to have reserves of uncommitted strength.[46]

For Rabi, Hinduism appealed to Oppenheimer specifically because Eastern faiths went beyond dogma and theology, leaving greater possibilities for exploration and interpretation. But Hinduism, with strong concepts of duty and fate, would also be a tool for negotiating his own relationship to one of the most destructive acts in human history.

Beyond Hinduism, Oppenheimer also found moral inspiration in canonical works of great literature. Defining titles for him included Dostoevsky's *Crime and Punishment* (1866) and *The Brothers Karamazov* (1880), the poetry of John Donne, and Proust's *À la recherche du temps perdu* (1913). In 1963, Oppenheimer was asked by *The Christian Century* magazine to list the books that had had a shaping effect on his 'vocational attitude' and on his 'philosophy of life'. The ten titles he chose were:

Les Fleurs du Mal (The Flowers of Evil)
    by Charles Baudelaire (1857)
The Waste Land by T.S. Eliot (1922)
The Divine Comedy by Dante Alighieri (1321)

Bhagavad Gita Satakatraya ('The Three Centuries')
   by Bhartrihari (5th century CE)
Hamlet by William Shakespeare (1623)
L'Éducation sentimentale ('Sentimental Education')
   by Gustave Flaubert (1869)
The Collected Works of Bernhard Riemann
   by Bernhard Riemann (1876)
Theaetetus by Plato (4th century BCE)
Faraday's Diary, Being the Various Philosophical Notes
   of Experimental Investigation made by Michael Faraday
   by Michael Faraday (1933)

This selection is wide-ranging in genre and subject, journeying from canonical works of Western literature such as *Hamlet* and *The Waste Land* to niche scientific books, taking a detour through Christian and Eastern religion along the way. We can also read the list against Oppenheimer's interest in the investigations and solutions of modern psychoanalysis – taken collectively, many of the works sit on the borderlands between faith, reason and psychology. Rabi commented that '[Wolfgang] Pauli once remarked to me that Oppenheimer seemed to treat physics as an avocation and psychoanalysis as a vocation.'[47] Given the undeniable psychiatric problems Oppenheimer had experienced personally, it is little wonder that he came to understand life as a struggle through a challenging mental landscape. He personally visited psychoanalysts to confront his own demons, and many of the people in his life were engaged in deep psychological struggles. His developing interest in the human mind, its randomness and function, became another tool for Oppenheimer to understand the complex moral and personal story developing around him.

One rumour about Oppenheimer needs laying to rest. During the early 1940s, Oppenheimer's colleague Leonard Loeb, a Swiss-born American physicist, claimed that Oppenheimer had pursued a homosexual relationship with one of his PhD students, Harvey Hall. There is almost certainly no substance to this claim. Both men went on to be married with children; that in itself is not a conclusive proof, but combined with the paucity of supporting evidence the rumour seems more likely the product of resentful minds.

SCIENTIFIC PROGRESS

The 1930s were arguably the most exciting time in history to be a physicist. Every year seemed to bring new breakthroughs among the global physics community. Each fresh insight provided intellectual fuel to Oppenheimer and his teams, and thus the decade was especially fruitful in terms of Oppenheimer's personal research.

Oppenheimer could, as we have seen, be prone to error, particularly in some of his earlier papers. For instance, on 7 May 1931 Oppenheimer and Hall published their two-part paper 'Relativistic Theory of the Photoelectric Effect' in *Physical Review*. The paper was the basis of Hall's PhD, and among other contentions it developed 'A strict theory of the absorption of x-rays is developed on the basis of relativistic quantum electrodynamics. The theory is applied to the absorption of x-rays by a Dirac electron in the field of a nucleus.'[48] It was an important paper in an equally important field, but Hall and Oppenheimer's arguments were undermined by mathematical errors. Working in a fast-moving field, Oppenheimer also came tantalizingly close to making key breakthroughs in particle physics but was beaten to the finish line. Building upon Dirac's work, in 1930 Oppenheimer published 'On the theory of electrons and protons', in which he developed a promising theory that hinted at the existence of a new particle with the same mass as an electron but with a positive charge (electrons have a negative charge). It would be the physicist Carl Anderson, however, who confirmed the existence of the 'positron' in 1932. Like so many of Oppenheimer's peers, Anderson would go on to receive the Nobel Prize in Physics, an honour that despite Oppenheimer's prolific and important output eluded him throughout his career. Hans Bethe, however, later said that Oppenheimer's 1930 paper 'essentially predicted the positive electron'.[49]

One area in which Oppenheimer did blaze a trail in theoretical physics was his research into 'cosmic rays' – high-energy particles that had been detected entering Earth's atmosphere from space. Different theories regarding the nature of these rays had emerged among the international physics community. One of the most influential came from Robert Millikan, who also happened to be the chairman of the Executive Council (the governing body) of Caltech, so held at least a positional authority in relation to Oppenheimer. Millikan argued that cosmic rays were actually photons created by the birth of new matter, a process that by philosophical by-product also proved the existence of a creative God. Oppenheimer publicly and convincingly disagreed with this theory, earning himself Millikan's lasting antipathy, adding to a small but steadily growing list of those ill-disposed towards Oppenheimer.

New discoveries in physics came thick and fast during the early 1930s, constantly changing frameworks and challenging existing understanding. In May 1932, James Chadwick revolutionized par-

In this photograph taken at Caltech on 28 May 1935, Oppenheimer stands alongside Nobel Prize winners Robert Millikan (centre) and Paul Dirac (left). Oppenheimer himself never received the Nobel Prize.

ticle physics through his discovery of the neutron, an uncharged particle that along with protons make up the nucleus of an atom. In 1934, Italian-American physicist Enrico Fermi gave a solid theoretical framework for the existence of the 'neutrino', an uncharged subatomic particle first postulated by Wolfgang Pauli; experimental evidence for the existence of the neutrino only came in 1956. The deepening insight into atomic structure, plus advances in atomic experimentation such as Lawrence's invention of the cyclotron, led to the theoretical understanding that atoms, historically regarded as permanent and indivisible, could potentially be split. The theory was confirmed experimentally on 14 April 1932 at the

Cavendish laboratory by physicists John Cockcroft and Ernest Walton, who fired protons at lithium atoms, the splitting of which also revealed the potential release of vast amounts of energy. The results of this experimentation were announced by Rutherford later in the month, to much international press attention. Strategy and science met in the possibility of producing a weapon unrivalled in the already dire history of human violence.

Oppenheimer, meanwhile, was preoccupied in important work in the field of quantum electrodynamics, specifically working on reformulating Dirac's theory of the electron. He rarely worked alone, often producing papers in collaboration with his students or other leading physicists. His collaborative partners included Felix Bloch, Wendell Furry, Melba Phillips and Ernest Lawrence. His work with Phillips was especially productive and led to one of Oppenheimer's best-known contributions to physics – the Oppenheimer–Phillips Process – which explained the process of nuclear fusion that occurred in stars, an activity with a fundamental relation to the structure of the universe.

But Oppenheimer's intellectual particles were only just beginning to accelerate, and by the end of the 1930s he had produced further theories that would shape modern physics and which still have validity and influence to this day. The years 1938 and 1939 were key in this regard, specifically in the field of astrophysics. Oppenheimer was a wide-ranging theoretical physicist, but by this stage of his career it was astrophysics, a discipline that sat at the crossroads of classical physics and quantum mechanics, that was dominating his attention. He had a productive partner in this endeavour in Russian-Canadian physicist George Volkoff, who came to Berkeley in 1936 to escape Soviet persecution, settling

Top: Oppenheimer's bushy hairstyle separates him out in the second row of this photograph, taken at a University of Minnesota physics symposium in 1931. Above: The staff of the Radiation Laboratory at Berkeley National Laboratory pose under the magnet for a 60-inch cyclotron; Oppenheimer stands in the back row, centre.

in the USA and avoiding the Stalinist horrors that killed many of his family. In February 1939, Oppenheimer and Volkoff together published a paper entitled 'On Massive Neutron Cores'. In it, they presented the mathematical theory of neutron stars, super-dense celestial objects that are formed from the remnants of a massive star undergoing a supernova explosion, with the core of the star collapsing in on itself under intense gravitational forces. Oppenheimer had previously published a paper on neutron stars with Robert Serber, but his work with Volkoff had far greater vision and influence. Note, at this point in scientific history the existence of neutron stars was purely theoretical – it had not been confirmed empirically – but Oppenheimer and Volkoff defined the mathematical reality. Only in the 1960s and 1970s were neutron stars physically detected.

Oppenheimer followed his work on neutron stars with the paper 'On Continued Gravitational Contraction', co-authored with the mathematician Hartland Snyder and published in the *Physical Review* on 1 September 1939. The impact of the paper was undoubtedly reduced by its publication date coinciding with the German invasion of Poland, beginning the Second World War, but it was one of Oppenheimer's most significant contributions to physics, and therefore warrants quoting the paper's abstract:

> When all thermonuclear sources of energy are exhausted a sufficiently heavy star will collapse. Unless fission due to rotation, the radiation of mass, or the blowing off of mass by radiation, reduce the star's mass to the order of that of the sun, this contraction will continue indefinitely. In the present paper we study the solutions of the gravitational field equations which describe this process. In

I, general and qualitative arguments are given on the behavior of the metrical tensor as the contraction progresses: the radius of the star approaches asymptotically its gravitational radius; light from the surface of the star is progressively reddened, and can escape over a progressively narrower range of angles. In II, an analytic solution of the field equations confirming these general arguments is obtained for the case that the pressure within the star can be neglected. The total time of collapse for an observer comoving with the stellar matter is finite, and for this idealized case and typical stellar masses, of the order of a day; an external observer sees the star asymptotically shrinking to its gravitational radius.[50]

The language and concepts are challenging for the layman, but essentially Oppenheimer is here predicting the existence of what today we call 'black holes'. These are regions in space formed when massive stars collapse under their own gravity at the end of their life cycle. The force of gravity at this point is so strong that nothing, not even light itself, can escape from it once light has passed the gravitational boundary known as the 'event horizon'. This paper not only established the 'Oppenheimer–Snyder Model' for representing the dynamics of stellar collapse and the formation of black holes, but it also advanced the understanding of Einstein's theory of general relativity and the behaviour of objects under massive gravitation. The American theoretical physicist Jeremy Bernstein referred to this paper as 'one of the great papers in twentieth-century physics'.[51]

Biographer Ray Monk has pointed to the fact that Oppenheimer's great papers of 1939 remained relatively obscure for many decades, the theoretical work rather under-appreciated until the actual existence of neutron stars and black holes were confirmed in the 1960s and 1970s. This work should remind us, however, that Oppenheimer's lifetime efforts should not purely be circumscribed by his involvement in the Manhattan Project.

POLITICAL LEANINGS

The 1930s represent an ideological turning point in the life of J. Robert Oppenheimer. During this time, the gravity of global events compressed his previously diffuse world-view into a more defined identity. The ideological journey he embarked upon would later be profoundly consequential for him personally, when exposed under the harsh spotlight of Cold War politics.

The 1930s were a convulsive time in international strategic relations. The world was still clawing its way out of the financial agonies of the Great Depression and the social and political consequences of a global war. The Russian Revolution of 1917 was in the process of redrawing the ideological map of the world; the battle lines between communism and capitalism were already being etched in physical borders and ideological hostilities. It was also a decade of fervent rising nationalism, especially in Germany, Italy and Japan, countries that were sowing the seeds of future war with their fusion of nationalism, militarism and imperialism.

Up until this time, Oppenheimer had never been the most politically engaged individual. But now, radical politics invaded even the siloed world of physics. Germany, for centuries one of Europe's intellectual leading lights, descended into the dark valley as Adolf Hitler and his Nazi Party came to power in 1933. Hitler's extreme anti-Semitism meant that overnight many of Germany's great scientists became pariahs in their own nation. In April

1933, the first anti-Jewish laws were promulgated, which included stripping all 'non-Aryan' academics of their teaching and research posts. A full 25 per cent of German physicists, including 11 past or future Nobel Prize winners, lost their jobs. Under such vicious constraints, which would only tighten, many scientists opted for emigration while they could. The list of those who fled reads like a roll-call of the 20th century's most influential physicists: Albert Einstein, Max Born, James Franck, Eugene Wigner, Leo Szilard, John von Neumann, Hans Bethe, Edward Teller, Joseph Rotblat, Wolfgang Pauli. Leading institutions, including Göttingen, were left intellectually gutted.

The international community, but especially the USA and the UK, made efforts to receive the German brain drain, as much for scientific self-interest as for altruism. The result was a cognitive migration that would, ultimately, have a profound bearing on the final outcome of the approaching world war. In the USA, Jewish scientists were received at a select group of universities, especially those resistant to America's own prevailing anti-Semitism, and included Caltech and Princeton.

As a Jewish scientist, albeit secularized, and one familiar with Germany's august scientific traditions, Oppenheimer was moved by the horror unfolding in Europe. The persecution of the Jews spurred a political awakening, broadening into a more generalized interest in social justice. During the AEC security commission hearings in 1954, Oppenheimer confessed that until around the mid-1930s his political radar had been effectively switched off: 'I was almost wholly divorced from the contemporary scene in this country. I never read a newspaper or a current magazine like *Time* or *Harper's*; I had no radio, no telephone; I learned of the stock market crash in the fall of 1929 only long after the event; the first time I ever voted was in the presidential election of 1936.'[52] But the rise of Nazism was a personal watershed, a filter through which the world was now changed utterly:

> I had a continuing, smoldering fury about the treatment of Jews in Germany. I had relatives there, and was later to help in extricating them and bringing them to this country. I saw what the Depression was doing to my students... And through them, I began to understand how deeply political and economic events could affect men's lives.[53]

Going forward, Oppenheimer began to embrace activism, at least on a scale that was comfortable to him. Since he was financially secure, much of his activism would be expressed in the form of monetary contributions. In December 1933, for example, Oppenheimer received a letter sent to targeted American intellectuals, encouraging them to give financial support to German physicists who had lost their livelihoods in the Nazi purge – Oppenheimer accordingly gave about 3 per cent of his salary to this cause.

Oppenheimer's push-back against anti-Semitism has, however, received far less interest than his progressive journey into left-wing politics. Historically, the USA has had a difficult and, periodically, combative relationship with left-wing ideology, but the historical big picture can obscure the rowdy excitement of socialism and communism in the American culture of the 1930s. From working-class labour unions to radicalized academia, many US individuals and groups embraced what they saw as communism's idealism, an end to capitalist exploitation. Hostility towards communism was undoubtedly pronounced, especially in traditional American society and mainstream politics, but there was not quite yet the 'red scare' ultra-paranoia of the 1950s. Many stateside socialists and communists even felt that left-wing ideologies were actually the fulfilment of American, constitutional values, the desire to release *all* peoples into the sunlit uplands of the American dream. Socially, Oppenheimer was effectively swimming in a sea of left-wing influences. Many of his students and research associates were already committed members of the CPUSA by the mid-1930s, and their world-view began to rub off on Oppenheimer.

Given the later hysteria about communism, we need to tread carefully when attempting to define Oppenheimer's relationship to left-wing politics. Certainly, some of his closest associates had radical leanings. In 1934 the physicist Robert Serber arrived at Berkeley, along with his wife Charlotte. Serber had a soaring intellect, one that would play an important role in the later Manhattan Project, and he and Oppenheimer became firm friends. Although neither Serber nor Charlotte appear to have been actual members of the Communist Party (unlike Charlotte's brother and sister), they had definite left-wing leanings. Others in Oppenheimer's circle took a deeper plunge. One such individual was Wendell Furry, with whom Oppenheimer wrote the paper 'On the Theory of the Electron and Positive' in 1934. While at Harvard that same year, Furry became a fully subscribed communist. He would pay a harsh price for his beliefs in the 1950s, under the interrogations of McCarthyism, although at that time he refused to take the Fifth Amendment as many others had, and instead chose to defend his beliefs publicly, a psychologically punishing route to take.

Oppenheimer's beloved brother Frank also embraced communism. For Oppenheimer, this brought left-wing ideology closer to home, as from 1935 Frank attended Caltech as a doctoral student in physics. Frank was far more politically stirred than his brother, animated by left-wing doctrine, causes and society. His embrace of communism was encouraged when, in the spring of 1936, he met Berkeley graduate student Jacquenette ('Jackie') Quann, a radical working-class French-Canadian who had joined the Young Communist League during her undergraduate years. They fell in love, a briskly paced romance that led to marriage on 15 September 1936 (Frank evidently chose to ignore his brother's historic advice about avoiding women). Oppenheimer, however, neither approved of the marriage nor of Frank's chosen bride. In his security hearings testimony of 1954, Oppenheimer wrote that 'My brother Frank married in 1936. Our relations were inevitably less intimate than before.'[54] Oppenheimer regarded Jackie with condescension, referring to her as 'the waitress my brother married'[55] – as with so many upper-class leftists of the 1930s, a love of the working class in general often didn't extend to the working class in particular. Robert was also likely upset when both Frank and Jackie became members of the CPUSA between 1937 and 1939. Whatever sympathies Oppenheimer might have had towards communist goals, he was also aware that being a visible member of the party would do Frank's future job prospects no favours. Nor was Frank a passive member. He attended party meetings and also formed a secretive group of communist scientists at Caltech.

When we turn our attention from friends, associates and family to Oppenheimer himself, his relationship to communism is nuanced. Certainly, Oppenheimer appears drawn to explore the left-wing movements around him and connect with their prominent personalities. For example, Robert Serber remembered attending a union general strike protest in 1934, having been invited to the event by Oppenheimer, alongside Charlotte Serber and Melba Phillips. Oppenheimer also went to one of Frank's Communist Party house meetings, although later shrugged off that event, saying that the 'meeting made no detailed impression on me'.[56]

That particular meeting might have been less than inspiring, but during the second half of the 1930s Oppenheimer's interest in communism deepened, as did his participation in its local community. And here romance played its part. By the autumn of 1936, Oppenheimer, like many Western intellectuals, was gripped by events in Spain, now engulfed in an agonizing and enormously destructive civil war between left-wing Republicans and right-wing Nationalists. Thousands of foreigners crossed oceans and continents to join the Republican fight – here, they believed, was the literal frontline between communism and fascism, and many wanted to be part of the heroic struggle. At one fund-raising meeting, Oppenheimer met a similarly inspired 22-year-old medical student, Jean Tatlock. The captivation was instant. Tatlock was a beauty, her dark, short-cut wavy hair framing hazel-blue eyes, strong eyebrows and gracefully curved red lips. Apart from the Spanish Republican cause, it soon became clear they shared other interests – Freud, Jung, Donne. The chemistry between them was immediate and they soon began dating.

It was to be a passionate relationship. It was also intense and volatile. Tatlock, herself determined to become a psychiatrist, was also a highly troubled young woman, potentially suffering from bipolar disorder or manic depression. There is also evidence suggesting that she was a lesbian, a sexual orientation that in the 1930s was something to suppress and not embrace, with all the resulting tensions that brought with it. Whatever inner battle Tatlock fought, it expressed itself openly in her relationship with Oppenheimer. Her feelings for him and her behaviour towards him rose and fell in waves, one day craving his attention, the next rejecting any contact. She could be cruel to him verbally, scornful. Oppenheimer poured fuel on the fire with obsessional behaviour, constantly buying Tatlock flowers and gifts, tokens that seem to have infuriated Tatlock rather than consoled her.

Oppenheimer's volatile romance coincided with another important event in his life. On 20 September 1937, Julius Oppenheimer died from a heart attack. The family loss was partly counterbalanced by the arrival from Germany of Hedwig Stern, Julius' younger sister, plus her son Alfred. The pair of immigrants settled in safety in Berkeley; Oppenheimer became especially fond of his aunt.

Julius Oppenheimer's demise meant that he was thus spared much of the drama produced by Oppenheimer's relationship with Tatlock. It was one with a distinct political dimension. Tatlock, despite hailing from an elite academic family, was an active, albeit erratic, communist. She had joined the Communist Party in 1933–34 while at Berkeley, writing articles for the party newspaper *Western Worker*. Oppenheimer's relationship with Tatlock drew him deeper into leftist circles, as he explained to the AEC hearings in 1954, in a letter to Major General Kenneth D. Nichols, the general manager of the AEC:

> In the spring of 1936, I had been introduced by friends to Jean Tatlock, the daughter of a noted professor of English at the university

[Chaucer scholar John S.P. Tatlock]; and in the autumn, I began to court her, and we grew close to each other. We were at least twice close enough to marriage to think of ourselves as engaged. Between 1939 and her death in 1944 I saw her very rarely. She told me about her Communist Party memberships; they were on again, off again affairs, and never seemed to provide for her what she was seeking. I do not believe that her interests were really political. She loved this country and its people and its life. She was, as it turned out, a friend of many fellow travelers and Communists, with a number of whom I was later to become acquainted. I should not give the impression that it was wholly because of Jean Tatlock that I made leftwing friends, or felt sympathy for causes which hitherto would have seemed so remote from me, like the Loyalist cause in Spain, and the organization of migratory workers. I have mentioned some of the other contributing causes. I liked the new sense of companionship, and at the time felt that I was coming to be part of the life of my time and country.[57]

Oppenheimer chose his words carefully. Here he is keen to weaken the sincerity of her ideological commitment, painting communism more as a wavering flirtation, rising and falling with her mental state. He also expands on his acculturation to American communism through a variety of left-wing causes. The last sentence of this quotation is also important, because it gives one of the few direct statements of why Oppenheimer might have been drawn to communism. The 'companionship' and 'part of the life of my time and country' suggest that Oppenheimer found in the leftist community a sense of belonging, an integration that in some ways he had been seeking all his life.

We should not, however, take away the impression that communism was nothing more than a gentle comfort blanket for Oppenheimer. Taking the period 1937–42, other activities demonstrate a person making more practical contributions to the communist cause. Ray Monk has shown how Oppenheimer actually donated about $1,000 every year to his local Communist Party group, albeit with slight indirection through leftist-inspired causes, such as support for Spanish Republicans. Given that his annual salary was about $15,000 per annum, he was making a substantial contribution, not a casual donation.

Oppenheimer also began working for the communist-aligned Teachers' Union, which represented university educators, not just school teachers. Specifically, he was engaged as the 'recording secretary' of the Berkeley branch, headed by the charismatic, handsome French-Norwegian professor Haakon Chevalier. This man, above many others, would be an obsessional focus in the AEC's case against Oppenheimer in the 1950s; the association between the two men would hang heavy around Oppenheimer's neck. Haakon defended his own position in the post-war years by claiming that Oppenheimer was more than just an ideological dilettante. He claimed that in addition to the Teacher's Union role, Oppenheimer also became a member of a secret Communist Party 'unit' within Berkeley, consisting of six to ten influential individuals who met to discuss and plan the local party agenda.

Later, Oppenheimer fought back vigorously against accusations that he was a covert communist activist. He admitted that he 'had probably belonged to every communist-front organization on the west coast'[58], although he later retracted this comment as wry hyperbole. Given the full range of his associations and connections, it does seem that for a distinct period of his life (1936–41) Oppenheimer was intellectually involved in communism to an extent he later did not wish to confess. But taking his life in its totality, which involves allowing a person to evolve and change, we don't get the sense that Oppenheimer was at any stage a communist subversive. Rather, he was someone who found in communism a set of perspectives that connected with a more general, idealistic political awakening. Furthermore, his affinity for left-wing ideology did not survive the sociopathic reality of Soviet communism, once the depths of its cruelty were exposed. On 23 August 1939, the Soviet Union signed a non-aggression pact with Nazi Germany, then invaded Poland from the east on 17 September. Oppenheimer saw clearly how Soviet actions hollowed out many of communism's claims to the moral high ground in international politics. He also recognized that communist credentials would hobble his career advancement, so backed away from active involvement in communist circles.

His romantic life, as ever, complicated the picture. Oppenheimer's tortured relationship with Tatlock struggled and fizzled out, leaving him open to new possibilities. In the summer of 1939, he met one Katherine Puening Harrison, aka 'Kitty', at a house party. Kitty was a married woman; her husband was Richard Stewart Harrison, a physicist at Caltech. Richard was actually Kitty's third husband, and by the time she met Oppenheimer at the party this marriage was already struggling for survival.

Kitty's background was profoundly different to that of Oppenheimer's. German-born, with a blue-blood aristocratic ancestry on her mother's side (she was related to both King Albert I of Belgium and Britain's Queen Victoria), Kitty had emigrated to the

USA when she was two, along with her family. Her first marriage was to a Frank Ramseyer, an American studying music in Paris; this marriage was annulled when Kitty discovered that her partner was inconveniently both homosexual and a drug user. Her second marriage took a quite different direction with Joseph Dallet Jr., a communist activist and union organizer. This relationship was full of passion and ideas, but it brought with it a working-class reality Kitty was ill-suited to endure. The couple at one point were reduced to living on benefits that amounted to $12.50 each per month. But she was drawn to the cause, and became a member of the CPUSA, with duties that included selling the *Daily Worker* newspaper on the city streets. Kitty's leftist political choices, as with those of Oppenheimer, would come back to haunt her. But it soon became clear that the life of an impoverished activist was not for her, and Kitty and Dallet parted ways in June 1936. Dallet was later killed fighting in the Spanish Civil War.

Kitty met her third husband, Harrison, in Philadelphia, where she had enrolled at the University of Pennsylvania. There they also met Robert and Charlotte Serber. It was that couple who provided the interface between Kitty and Oppenheimer.

The party at which they met triggered a rapid-onset romance. In the summer of 1940 Oppenheimer even took her to stay in *Perro Caliente*, to meet Frank and Jackie. Aware of the optics, Oppenheimer told his brother and wife that Harrison simply couldn't make it. Jackie did not warm to Kitty. In fact, she detested her, quickly coming to regard her as a 'phoney', 'schemer' and 'bitch'.[59] She would not be alone in this reaction. During the Los Alamos years, Kitty was thoroughly disliked by many, some grading her as positively evil. But clearly Oppenheimer didn't see it that way, testified by the awkward fact that Kitty soon became pregnant with Oppenheimer's child. A divorce from Richard was hastily arranged, and on 1 November 1940 Kitty and Oppenheimer were married. A baby boy, Peter, arrived on 12 May 1941, much to Oppenheimer's delight.

By this time, Kitty was no longer a member of the CPUSA, but she still had a rich portfolio of communist and leftist friends, a fact that hardly made Oppenheimer's future simpler. She was especially close with the CPUSA's San Francisco branch chairman, Steve Nelson, a full-blown communist operator trained in Moscow and subsequently employed on espionage missions. She also knew well William Schneiderman, the San Francisco branch's secretary and a known agitator. The Federal Bureau of Investigation (FBI), who would become Oppenheimer's constant state shadow, had both men under tight surveillance. On one occasion, agents were monitoring a communist meeting at Schneiderman's house, taking details of the cars parked outside. One of them belonged to Oppenheimer. It is clear that Oppenheimer's new wife, like Tatlock, was going to add to Oppenheimer's increasingly thick folder in the FBI's anti-communism filing cabinets.

GOING ATOMIC

Oppenheimer's interest in nuclear physics emerges around 1934. By this stage in the history of physics, many of the foundations of atomic theory had already been laid. The work of pioneers such as Rutherford, Blackett and Cockcroft between 1919 and 1932 had clarified fundamental atomic physics and had split an atom, but only in terms of simple elements. In 1934, the Italian-American physicist Enrico Fermi induced radioactivity by bombarding elements with neutrons, leading to the discovery of new elements and providing a deeper understanding of nuclear reactions.

In 1938, the German scientists Otto Hahn and Fritz Strassmann began conducting experiments firing slow neutrons targeting uranium atoms. Hahn and Strassmann noted that the output of their experiments was the production of barium, which from a mathematical perspective made no sense in terms of the energy lost and gained in the process. Hahn sent his results to a friend, Austrian-Swedish physicist Lise Meitner, who with her colleague (and nephew) Otto Frisch discovered that the uranium atom had been split through the process of fission. That process, in turn, delivered vast amounts of energy by releasing the binding energy that held the uranium nuclei together. Startled and excited by the findings, Meitner published the results in *Nature*, and directed them to Niels Bohr in Copenhagen. From here the discoveries, and speculations about their potential, began to work their way out to the international physics community. Niels Bohr and colleague Léon Rosenfeld took the insights to the USA, disseminating them via contacts in Princeton and other research institutions.

The theoretical and experimental understanding of nuclear fission metaphorically exploded among the American physics community with the force it portended. It was the literal embodiment of Einstein's theory of the equivalence between mass and energy. Oppenheimer joined in the general excitement. His letters, lectures and seminars of the late 1930s showed that he quickly grasped the leap from the theoretical possibilities of fission to the practical potential for both energy generation and weaponization. The dire vision of atomic weaponry had been described as far back as 1913 by English writer H.G. Wells, but now it was shifting from science fiction to practical challenge. Oppenheimer's reaction to developments was later recounted in Robert Serber's autobiography: 'Oppie would write to me every Sunday. From one of those Sunday letters, which I received in January 1939, I learned of the discovery of fission. In that first letter Oppie mentioned the possibility of nuclear power and of an explosive.'[60]

The practical strategies for developing an atomic weapon began to crystallize, at least in thought, from 1939. Niels Bohr and Princeton's Archibald Wheeler together outlined the Bohr–Wheeler theory of nuclear fission, which identified a rare isotope of uranium, U-235, as the optimal element for the fission process. This discovery, as we shall see, was critical to the future Manhattan Project. The most common form of uranium, U-238, constitutes 99.3 per cent of natural uranium, with U-235 consisting of the scant 0.7 per cent remaining. Therefore, the process of extracting U-235 in sufficient quantities, quickly enough, would become one of the defining theoretical and engineering challenges of the atomic bomb project. Lawrence began working on this challenge in early 1941, using an electromagnetic process, and Oppenheimer assisted him in this endeavour.

Building on the Bohr–Wheeler theory, physicists in the USA, Britain and Europe began expending vast intellectual effort trying to crack the practical secrets of fission, which were legion. Oppenheimer was drawn steadily into the orbit of this work, which he found absorbing. He became particularly focused on questions regarding whether 'fast' or 'slow' neutrons would be optimal for generating the fission reaction in uranium. Much investigation lay ahead for Oppenheimer and others before that clarification came.

One of the most significant developments in the history of atomic weaponry came in March 1939. The Hungarian-born physicist Leo Szilard had modelled a neutron-induced nuclear chain reaction back in 1934; indeed, he had filed a patent for the concept in March that year (the patent was granted). In 1939 Szilard's later experiments, working at Columbia University with the likes of Walter Zinn, John Dunning, Enrico Fermi and Herbert L. Anderson, confirmed the theoretical feasibility of an atomic weapon. Szilard recognized that this was the beginning of the ultimate arms race, was deeply troubled, and felt compelled to act. Szilard and Einstein, assisted by Eugene Wigner and Edward Teller, composed a letter – signed by Einstein to give it maximum leverage – to President Franklin D. Roosevelt, warning of the dangers the world now faced. The letter was delivered to the White House in August 1939 and made its way to the President's desk by the following October. Read in the context of the war that was now raging in Europe, the letter was clear about what was at stake:

In the course of the last four months it has been made probable – through the work of Joliot in France as well as Fermi and Szilard in America – that it may become possible to set up a nuclear chain reaction in a large mass of uranium, by which vast amounts of power and large quantities of new radium-like elements would be generated. Now it appears almost certain that this could be achieved in the immediate future.

This new phenomenon would also lead to the construction of bombs, and it is conceivable – though much less certain – that extremely powerful bombs of a new type may thus be constructed.

> A single bomb of this type, carried by boat and exploded in a port, might very well destroy the whole port together with some of the surrounding territory. However, such bombs might very well prove to be too heavy for transportation by air.[61]

The letter also made the loaded observation that 'Germany has actually stopped the sale of uranium from the Czechoslovakian mines which she has taken over'. The clear implication was that Germany might have a head start in the atomic future.

The letter caught Roosevelt's attention. In October 1939, he authorized the formation of a presidential Committee on Uranium, purposed to evaluate and co-ordinate research into atomic weaponry. Among its small group of experts were Szilard, Wigner and Teller. As the importance of the work become more elevated, however, this underfunded body mutated into the more muscular Section on Uranium (S-1) in the newly created Office of Scientific Research and Development (OSRD), headed by Vannevar Bush, who was already the chairman of the National Advisory Committee for Aeronautics (NACA) and the National Defense Research Committee (NDRC). The latter was absorbed into the OSRD, and its remit, to organize American science for the war effort, was to be handled by Bush's capable deputy, organic chemistry expert James Conant. The OSRD began to receive substantial funding. Its efforts were also galvanized by those of the British MAUD Committee, also dedicated to atomic bomb research. The MAUD scientists had concluded in March 1941 that an atomic bomb was practically viable, with just several kilograms of uranium potentially sufficient to wipe out a small city. The race for the atomic bomb would soon become the biggest single defence investment in American history.

In January 1942, Nobel Prize-winning physicist Arthur H. Compton was given responsibility for co-ordinating the US national efforts to build a fully functioning atomic bomb, through a Chicago-based organization called the Metallurgical Laboratory, but with satellite labs across the USA. Here Oppenheimer enters our story. On 21 October 1941, Oppenheimer had attended a conference in Schenectady, New York, his presence at the insistence of Lawrence. The main topic of discussion was the possibility of using fast neutrons for the fission process. Crucially, Oppenheimer developed a working estimate of the amount of U-235 required to maintain a self-sustaining fission chain reaction. Soon after the conference, Lawrence recommended Oppenheimer's work to Compton, who promptly gave Oppenheimer responsibility for fast-neutron research at Berkeley.

Oppenheimer seized the opportunity with gusto. These were the early days of the atomic project. The searing deaths of thousands was an outcome so distant, so separated by immense scientific challenges (many still thought an atomic bomb was not possible), that individuals like Oppenheimer could throw themselves into the effort motivated mostly by the opportunity to work on inexhaustibly funded cutting-edge science. To give the work his full attention, Oppenheimer resigned from his teaching position at Caltech, adding his capacious intelligence to the growing body of scientists employed by the OSRD. What began as a science project began to gather the olive-drab hue of a military project. On 8 October 1942, Oppenheimer met one Brigadier General Leslie Groves, commander of the project that would come to define the life of J. Robert Oppenheimer. It was called the Manhattan Project.

CHAPTER 4

LOS ALAMOS AND THE ATOMIC BOMB

The ambition of the Manhattan Project remains astonishing. Initially seeded in the early 1940s by a small group of forward-thinking scientists, at its peak it employed more than 150,000 people, although the total number involved across the lifetime of the project possibly exceeded 500,000. The scientific challenges posed by the Manhattan Project were vast and constant, frequently pushing experimental and theoretical physics beyond their predicted limits. Yet the project was much more than just a scientific venture. It required equally Herculean efforts in multiple domains: engineering, logistics, construction, administration, security, transport, communications, finance. By the end of the Second World War, the project's expenditure had reached $2 billion, equivalent to about $37 billion today. Its success was never guaranteed; indeed, on many occasions it hung in the balance.

More than anywhere else, J. Robert Oppenheimer made his mark on history via his role in the Manhattan Project. Although the project encompassed dozens of sites across the USA, it was concentrated in three major locations. The Oak Ridge, Tennessee, facility was dedicated to enriching uranium (i.e. processing uranium to make it capable of achieving nuclear fission). Meanwhile, the Hanford site in Washington was responsible for converting uranium into plutonium, another fissile material. These two sites constituted the largest portions of the Manhattan Project. However, the scientific and practical tip of the spear was at Los Alamos, New Mexico, where bomb design and testing were carried out. It was here that Oppenheimer, serving as the technical director, shouldered responsibilities few of us can conceive.

TAKING CHARGE

The Manhattan Project was born on 16 August 1942. The document that authorized the programme, War Department Order No. 33, made no mention of an atomic bomb, but cloaked its purpose in a more banal order – the creation of a new Corps of Engineering district, headquartered in New York. The establishment of the Manhattan District was doubly misleading, as in reality the Manhattan Project would have no geographical boundaries within the USA.

Oppenheimer (left) and other 'notable persons' at Oak Ridge

The man appointed to head the Manhattan Project was Colonel Leslie Groves, who was promoted to the rank of brigadier general upon his accession to the post. Groves was an army engineer officer to his core, resolute in mind, large in body (he was more than 1.8 m /6 ft tall and of hefty build) and an intimidating but capable leader. He was a proven organizer of massive engineering and civil works projects. He had taken, for example, a central role in creating the accommodation and garrison facilities for the mass mobilization of the US Army in 1940 and had led the construction of that most iconic federal building, the Pentagon, from mid-1941. He was a man who got things done.

As Grove's character is so important to the Oppenheimer story, it is worth sketching it out in a little more depth. This is done succinctly by US Army officer Kenneth D. Nicholls, a district engineer on the Manhattan Project:

General Groves is the biggest S.O.B. I have ever worked for. He is most demanding. He is most critical. He is always a driver, never a praiser. He is abrasive and sarcastic. He disregards all normal organizational channels. He is extremely intelligent. He has the guts to make difficult, timely decisions. He is the most egotistical man I know. He knows he is right and so sticks by his decision. He abounds with energy and expects everyone to work as hard or even harder than he does.[62]

Given the aggressive drive inherent in Groves' character, we might expect that he and Oppenheimer would be as incompatible as magnets with like poles. By contrast, they forged a close and supportive professional partnership.

Groves was first introduced to Oppenheimer at a lunch in Berkeley on 8 October 1942. Groves' previous encounters with project scientists had by and large been awkward and suspicious, a clash of cultures between the military and the civilian. Groves had a clear objective – a working atomic bomb – and tried to nail down the practical steps and the feasible dates for its construction. The scientists, however, were often more focused on the fascinating intricacies of theory and experiments. Oppenheimer, conversely,

Leslie Groves and Robert Oppenheimer appear almost caught unawares by this photograph at Los Alamos in 1942. Although very different in character, they became firm friends.

presented a clearer vision of how the project could be organized and run, and was openly co-operative and respectful. During the 1954 AEC headings, Oppenheimer outlined his input into the early phases of the Manhattan Project. It is worth quoting some passages of his written explanation to demonstrate his fit for the collaborative leadership role, in which he excelled:

In late summer, after a review of the experimental work, I became convinced, as did others, that a major change was called for in the work on the bomb itself. We needed a central laboratory devoted wholly to this purpose, where people could talk freely with each other, where theoretical ideas and experimental findings could affect each other, where the waste and frustration and error of the many compartmentalized experimental studies could be eliminated, where we could begin to come to grips with chemical, metallurgical, engineering, and ordnance problems that had so far received no consideration. We therefore sought to establish this laboratory for a direct attack on all the problems inherent in the most rapid possible development and production of atomic bombs.

In the autumn of 1942 General Groves assumed charge of the Manhattan Engineer District. I discussed with him the need for an atomic bomb laboratory. There had been some thought of making this laboratory a part of Oak Ridge. For a time there was support for making it a military establishment in which key personnel would be commissioned as officers; and in preparation for this course I once went to the Presidio to take the initial steps toward obtaining a commission.

After a good deal of discussion with the personnel who would be needed at Los Alamos and with General Groves and his advisers, it was decided that the Laboratory should, at least initially, be a civilian establishment in a military post. While this consideration was going on, I had shown General Groves Los Alamos; and he almost immediately took steps to acquire the site.

In early 1943, I received a letter signed by General Groves and Dr. Conant, appointing me director of the laboratory, and outlining their conception of how it was to be organized and administered. The necessary construction and assembling of the needed facilities were begun. All of us worked in close collaboration with the engineers of the Manhattan District.[63]

Some points of this outline require elaboration. First, Oppenheimer's desire to remove 'compartmentalization' from the Manhattan Project was a significant early leadership position. The US military's desire to preserve secrecy meant that the original intention was to silo the scientists in discrete tasks that would, at the local level, not reveal too much of the overall project. It is true that the bulk of the workers on the Manhattan Project ultimately had no knowledge of the scientific work occurring, nor of the ultimate purpose. But Oppenheimer knew the world of science, and how scientific minds worked at optimal levels. His experience of theoretical and experimental physics told him that the best, fastest results would be gleaned through constant sharing, discussion and interaction. He convinced Groves on this point and thus the shackles were taken off the scientific collaboration. Oppenheimer would also persuade Groves that the scientific work at Los Alamos should be run as a civilian effort. Initially, the Manhattan Project was organized under strictly military structures and procedures – even the scientists were to be given commissions and ranks. But again, the cultural distinctions between scientists and soldiers were profound, and militarization became a sticking point for many academics, more content wearing lab coats than service dress. Oppenheimer found the right balance, the scientists working in the way they were used to, albeit under the directional drive of overall military command, and Oppenheimer mediating capably between the two.

The location for the bomb design and development was settled in December 1942. Groves, Oppenheimer and others went out on scouting trips to find an optimal site: remote but not prohibitively inaccessible; amenable to the construction of large-scale facilities; dependable weather; suitable areas of destructive testing. Oppenheimer guided the team towards his beloved New Mexico, first showing them the area around Jemez Springs in the Jemez Mountains, in the central part of the state. But eventually this was switched to the mesa around the Los Alamos Ranch School, a boys' school that soon received its eviction notice. Los Alamos thus began its journey from remote secret to one of the most well-known scientific sites in history.

Oppenheimer was appointed as scientific director of Los Alamos in February 1943, although by this time he had largely taken that responsibility on a de facto basis. On his shoulders weighed the responsibility for corralling the science and the scientists towards a manifested, undeniable conclusion – a working and deployable atomic bomb. A letter to Oppenheimer from Groves and Conant dated 25 February 1943 outlined the duties of the scientific director as follows:

III. Responsibilities of the Scientific Director.

1. He will be responsible for:

A. The conduct of the scientific work so that the desired goals as outlined by the Military Policy Committee are achieved at the earliest possible dates.

B. The maintenance of secrecy by the civilian personnel under his control as well as their families.

2. He will of course be guided in his determination of policies and courses of action by the advice of his scientific staff.

3. He will keep Dr. James B. Conant and General Groves informed to such an extent as is necessary for them to carry on the work which falls in their respective spheres. Dr. Conant will be available at any time for consultation on general scientific problems as well as to assist in the determination of definite scientific policies and research programs. Through Dr. Conant complete access to the scientific world is guaranteed.[64]

Oppenheimer's appointment as director at Los Alamos, however, was by no means a universally approved move. In fact, it seems to have been largely on account of the impulse and insight of Leslie Groves, who built up a successful personal relationship with

Oppenheimer. In the post-war period, aware that the 1954 security hearings had made his choice of Oppenheimer even more controversial, Groves outlined both his concerns and his reasoning in his insightful work *Now it can be told: The story of the Manhattan Project*, published in 1962. In the cons column of reasons not to appoint Oppenheimer, Groves noted that:

> … all his work had been purely theoretical and had not taken him much beyond the point of being able to make an educated guess at the force an atomic fission bomb could exert. Nothing had been done on such down-to-earth problems as how to detonate the bomb, or how to design it so that it could be detonated. Adding to my cause for doubt, no one with whom I talked showed any great enthusiasm about Oppenheimer as a possible director of the project.[65]

So, it is evident that Oppenheimer was by no means a shoo-in to the position. But Groves had studied, and discarded, other possibilities. Ernest Lawrence, for example, was an 'outstanding experimental physicist' but he could not be withdrawn from his work on the electromagnetic process. Compton had both the understanding of physics and was a capable administrator, but again he could not be spared from his existing work. Harold Urey, director of the Atomic Bomb Project at Columbia University, with responsibility for uranium isotope separation, was regarded as more of a (brilliant) chemist than a physicist. There were therefore people whom Groves considered for the director role, but whose existing work commitments or gaps in their abilities ruled them out.

Groves also thought Oppenheimer had two other deficiencies to be overcome. First, like Urey, 'he had almost no administrative experience of any kind'. Given that the Manhattan Project would be an epic exercise in micro- and macro-management, this was troubling. Second, he had not won a Nobel Prize, unlike so many other scientists on the project, including Lawrence, Urey and Compton. Groves explained that there was a 'strong feeling' among many of the top brains at Los Alamos that the director needed to have a Nobel Prize if he was going to command the respect of those he would lead. Thus there was 'considerable opposition' to appointing Oppenheimer to the role.

Having heard the cons, we might expect Groves to counterbalance them with the pros. But his account of why he ultimately chose Oppenheimer is surprisingly vague, especially bearing in mind that his book was written after the AEC security hearings, when Groves might be expected to drive home the clarity behind his decision. He stated that the main reason Oppenheimer was appointed to the role was that 'it became apparent that we were not going to find a better man' – an ambiguous endorsement. But ultimately Groves based his decision on an astute judge of character, seeing in Oppenheimer the potential for the right sort of leadership, the optimal combination of intellect, persuasion and drive to inspire the scientists while pushing them to get the job done. The fact that Oppenheimer did not have a Nobel Prize, furthermore, was likely in his favour, given that Groves seemed to feel intellectually challenged by the brilliant minds around him. Oppenheimer treated Groves as an equal partner on the project, and loyalty – as every military man knows – is part of the glue that holds a military operation together.

CLEARED FOR DUTY

There were some other problems surrounding Oppenheimer's appointment, not least the issue of security. Even as he took on the role of scientific director, Oppenheimer had no official security clearance. Neither was obtaining that clearance a done deal, not least because Oppenheimer was a person held under relentless suspicion by several agencies, specifically: the Federal Bureau of Investigation (FBI) led by J. Edgar Hoover; the US Army's G-2 counter-intelligence section, led by Major General George Strong, but with Lieutenant Colonel Boris Pash as the head of West Coast operations (under which Los Alamos fell); and the Manhattan Project's own internal security, headed by Lieutenant Colonel John Lansdale, with oversight of the scientists and technicians handled by Captain Peer de Silva.

All these men were single-minded anti-communists, thus Oppenheimer, in such an all-knowing role, was under special scrutiny. As were all the other scientists. Many of them were left-leaning, or simply had a civilian disregard for operational security, being more accustomed to scientific openness and international transparency. The history of the Manhattan Project subsequently revealed that concerns about security were by no means paranoia. There *were* spies in the Manhattan Project and the MAUD Committee, feeding information to the Soviets – impactful figures such as Klaus Fuchs and Theodore Hall – but it would take time and effort to root them out. Their identities would mainly come to light after the end of the war.

In March 1943, the FBI was ordered to stop conducting investigations into Oppenheimer by G-2, in a bid to protect the secrecy of the Manhattan Project, such was its gravity. But the FBI's monitoring of other left-wing figures meant that Oppenheimer gave them additional material for their files. Pash also put Oppenheimer under near round-the-clock surveillance, which extended to tapping his phone and bugging his home and cars with listening devices.

The volume of surveillance produced some potential smoking guns. First, the FBI observed a meeting between Joe Weinberg, an ex-student of Oppenheimer who became a friend, and the afore-mentioned CPUSA leader Steve Nelson. Weinberg nervously shared some confidential information about the Manhattan Project, princi-pally relating to activities at Oak Ridge. Oppenheimer's name came up several times during the discussion. Yet while they spoke of the fact that Oppenheimer was *not* amenable to supplying information to the communists, for the FBI just the fact that his name was in the hat conferred guilt by association. The FBI's concerns were height-ened further when Nelson was subsequently observed meeting with Vasily Zubilin (real name Vasily Zarubin), a Soviet operative in the NKVD (People's Commissariat for Internal Affairs). Another recording of Nelson revealed him speaking of the development of an 'important weapon', and that he knew someone with communist sympathies working at high level on the project. He didn't name the individual, but Nelson referred to that person's involvement with the Teachers' Committee and the Spanish Committee, which led the FBI to conclude that individual was none other than Oppen-heimer. The FBI shared their information with Groves, Lansdale and Pash. The latter had his existing resistance to Oppenheimer's security clearance confirmed, but Groves and Lansdale felt that the evidence clearly demonstrated that Oppenheimer was definitely not a spy, so Oppenheimer ultimately received his security pass. He would, however, remain under watchful eyes.

Oppenheimer wearing his Los Alamos security badge.

The Nelson/Weinberg connection did not incriminate Oppenheimer convincingly. There was another incident, however, that would dog Oppenheimer well beyond the life of the Manhattan Project, one that he compounded through his own mishandling. Its origins lay in Berkeley, just before Oppenheimer moved to Los Alamos on 16 March 1943. In late 1942, Oppenheimer's friend and leftist Haakon Chevalier had been approached by a British communist resident in Berkeley, George Eltenton. Eltenton wanted to know if Chevalier could glean any information about the activities of the Radiation Laboratory (known as the 'Rad Lab') at Berkeley, a scientific institution with a strong connection to the work at Los Alamos. Eltenton asked Chevalier to approach Oppenheimer specifically and let him know that the Soviet consulate would be receptive to receiving any insights.

Chevalier followed through, making a veiled proposal to Oppenheimer during a house party, when they were alone in the kitchen. Oppenheimer pushed back immediately, stating 'But that is treason' and 'That is a terrible thing to do.'[66] The conversation ended quickly and Oppenheimer's unreserved pushback was conveyed to both Eltenton and Nelson. To make sure that the line was firmly drawn, Oppenheimer even met Nelson for lunch and spelled out his irrevocable drift away from communism. Oppenheimer was closing the door on his leftist past.

But that door stayed awkwardly ajar, especially in the minds of others. In August 1942, Pash identified one scientist in the Rad Lab under particular suspicion, the known communist Giovanni Rossi Lomanitz, who was also a close friend of Weinberg. Pash recommended that Lomanitz's existing deferment of military service be cancelled, so he could be removed from work on the atomic bomb and safely contained within a military unit. Oppenheimer opposed the move, and Pash summoned him to a meeting in San Francisco to discuss the matter.

Oppenheimer was a man of legendary intelligence, but on that day it seems to have failed him on many levels. He appeared eager to show Pash that he was finely tuned to security issues by telling him that he had been approached by an individual (Chevalier) who was interested in obtaining information to pass to the Soviet consulate. Pash was perturbed first by the fact that Oppenheimer did not relay this information to him earlier, but was more aggrieved when Oppenheimer resolutely refused to name the contact, although he did name Eltenton. Under Pash's intense questioning, Oppenheimer appears to have panicked (the transcript of this episode in the 1954 security hearings includes many pauses, digressions and ramblings). He told Pash that Eltenton had approached others: 'I have known two or three cases, and I think two of the men were with me at Los Alamos. They are men who are very closely associated with me.'[67] Pash was now champing at the bit to have all the names revealed, but Oppenheimer dug in. In fact, much later, during the security hearings, he revealed that this statement was in fact a complete fabrication, for reasons unclear even to himself: 'I was an idiot,' he offered.

The meeting in San Francisco ended badly. Pash was fired up, intent on getting to the truth. Oppenheimer was both submissive and evasive. Pash informed Lansdale and Groves about the meeting; they also confronted Oppenheimer, wanting the name of the contact. Still Oppenheimer demurred. He only released Chevalier's name finally in December 1943, after being ordered to do so directly by Groves. Clearly, Oppenheimer had generated a problem of his own making, and it would not be the end of the matter.

LIFE AT LOS ALAMOS

Security was the constant refrain at Los Alamos. This was not just a matter of guarding against spies and leaks. Oppenheimer was director of the most consequential military project in history. His personal safety and accountable movements, therefore, were a headache for General Groves, who did his level best to contain a spirit more used to complete freedom of movement, especially around New Mexico. One particular letter from Groves to Oppenheimer, writing in the summer of 1943, clearly shows Groves trying to inject some security discipline into Oppenheimer's day-to-day existence:

Day-to-day operations
July 29, 1943.
Dr. J. R. Oppenheimer
P. O. BOX 1663
Santa Fe. New Mexico

Dear Dr. Oppenheimer:

In view of the nature of the work on which you are engaged, the knowledge of it which is possessed by you and the dependence which rests upon you for its successful accomplishment, it seems necessary to ask you to take certain special precautions with respect to your personal safety.

It is requested that:
(a) You refrain from flying in airplanes of any description; the time saved is not worth the risk. (If emergency demands their use my prior consent should be requested.)
(b) You refrain from driving an automobile for any appreciable distance (above a few miles) and from being without suitable protection on any lonely road, such as the road from Los Alamos to Santa Fe. On such trips you should be accompanied by a competent, able bodied armed guard. There is no objection to the guard serving as chauffeur.
(c) Your cars should be driven with due regard to safety and that in driving about town a guard of some kind should be used, particularly during hours of darkness. The cost of such guard is a proper charge against the United States.

I realize that these precautions may be personally burdensome and that they may appear to you to be unduly restrictive but I am asking you to bear with them until our work is successfully complete.

Sincerely,
L. R. Groves
Brigadier General, C. E.[68]

To the reader today, there is some humour to be found in this letter

– the frustrated Groves was evidently aware of the terrible aban-
donment in Oppenheimer's driving. But it is also clear how utterly
central Groves felt Oppenheimer was to the ultimate success of the
work at Los Alamos; Oppenheimer is not merely another suit or
lab coat that could be easily replaced. The degree to which Oppenheimer complied with these requests is unclear. Given his love of
travel and exploration, he may well have been a hard individual
to rein in, although as the bomb began to take shape he certainly
grasped the gravity of his work.

Much of Oppenheimer's brainpower was absorbed with contributing to the construction of a facility at Los Alamos fit for a
cast of thousands. The barren expanse of New Mexico chosen for
the site had to be converted into not only a cutting-edge research
institute, but also all the accompanying infrastructure to create
what was, in effect, a sizeable town – housing, roads, electricity,
gas and water supply, schools (for the children of workers), shops,
postal services, etc. Although the physical heavy lifting and building were naturally handled by the Corps of Engineers, Oppenheimer was nevertheless a hands-on planner and administrator,
helping sort out the problems and adjustments of the many arriving scientists and their families.

There were, obviously, no explicit job advertisements posted
regarding the scientific work at Los Alamos. Oppenheimer was
therefore flat-out busy with the challenge of recruitment in the first
months. He travelled around the USA to acquire hand-picked talent, often emptying out university research labs in the process. Such
was Oppenheimer's status across the US scientific community, and
his superb powers of persuasion, that he drew in an unprecedented
corpus of talent. The scientists at Los Alamos would include indi-

viduals such as Luis Alvarez, Hans Bethe, Norris Bradbury, Enrico Fermi, Richard Feynman, Eric Jette, George Kistiakowsky, Seth Neddermeyer, John von Neumann, Emilio Segrè, Cyril Smith, Edward Teller, Victor Weisskopf, Robert Wilson and many others.

Oppenheimer was a crucial mediator between the sensibilities of the scientists and the time-driven demands of Groves. Oppenheimer had many qualities that made him eminently suitable for the work, not least his ability to absorb information at lightning speed from many sources and in many subjects, and synthesize it into a judicious course of action. Victor Weisskopf, a key scientist at Los Alamos, remembered Oppenheimer admiringly:

His uncanny speed in grasping the main point of any subject was a decisive factor; he could acquaint himself with the essential details of any part of the work. He did not direct from the head office. He was intellectually and even physically present at each decisive step. He was present in the laboratory or in the seminar rooms when a new effect was measured, when a new idea was conceived. It wasn't that he contributed so many ideas or suggestions; he did sometimes, but his main influence came from something else. It was his continuous and intense presence which produced a direct sense of participation in all of us; it created that unique atmosphere and challenge that prevailed in the place throughout its time.[69]

At Los Alamos, Oppenheimer clearly found his metier. He was also easy to spot. Initially, Oppenheimer conducted business while wearing a bold Stetson hat, but Groves basically ordered him to replace it with something less conspicuous, fearing that it would make him an easy target for assassins and spies. Oppenheimer begrudgingly complied, instead donning an unassuming wide-brimmed hat that became known, on account of the shape of the crown, as the 'pork-pie hat'. While this might have been more acceptable to Groves, over time the pork-pie hat became an iconic signature of Oppenheimer's public image. In May 1948, the very first issue of *Physics Today* had a cover image of nothing more than Oppenheimer's hat hanging from a piece of machinery; no explanatory text was needed for the public to know the hat's owner.

Life at Los Alamos for Oppenheimer was preoccupied, stimulating and exciting. For the Oppenheimer family in general, however, the picture was less than harmonious. Kitty, quite simply, did not warm to life at the base, with its rudimentary accommodation and strange rhythms. In fact, she came to loathe Los Alamos and her sidelined role in it. There was much loneliness on her part; Oppenheimer would work unflagging hours, leaving Kitty to manage a house and lifestyle not of her choosing. Her boredom found some

This picturesque cottage was home to the Oppenheimer family between 1942 and 1945 at Los Alamos.

short-term relief in a job as an on-site lab assistant, but eventually this fell by the wayside. She had few friends. Kitty Oppenheimer was known for being haughty and mercurial, affable one day and caustic and dismissive the next. Some even dramatically regarded her as approaching evil in character, thus she did not build a loyal social circle. Frank and Jackie Oppenheimer would join the work at Los Alamos in early 1945, but although they were family they certainly had little affection or time for Kitty.

Nor was motherhood much of a comfort to Kitty. In addition to their son Peter, the Oppenheimers also had a daughter called Katherine – known as 'Toni' – who arrived on 7 December 1944. Many accounts give the impression of two children neglected by distracted or depressed parents, compounded by the fact that Kitty had developed a heavy drinking habit. Jackie would remember grim afternoon 'cocktail parties', which basically involved Kitty sitting in a room in awkward silence, with a handful of subdued associates.

Of the two children, Toni seemed to come off worse, sometimes being left for days with a maid while Kitty travelled on shopping trips. This withdrawal reached a crescendo when Kitty went away to Pittsburgh with Peter for no less than three and a half months, leaving Toni with a family friend, Pat Sherr, who had recently suffered a miscarriage. Oppenheimer himself came to see Sherr on occasions; she noticed that he would sit and talk freely with her, but show little interest in seeing Toni. Then one day, Oppenheimer asked her if she would adopt Toni, explaining that 'I can't love her'. Sherr defensively turned down the offer.

During his first two years at Los Alamos, Oppenheimer also reignited a flame from his past. He connected again with Jean Tatlock, who was living in San Francisco and working as a child psy-

Top: Kitty Oppenheimer (left) with her children, Toni and Peter.
Above: Oppenheimer hosts a get-together at his home at Los Alamos, his guests including Victor Weisskopf (right), Dorothy McKibbin and Isidor Rabi.

chiatrist. Her communist connections meant that she, like Oppenheimer, remained of special interest to the FBI. Their surveillance of Tatlock meant that when Oppenheimer covertly entered her life again, their movements together were observed and recorded.

Oppenheimer had initially rejected a request from Tatlock that they meet up just before he left for Los Alamos. But in June 1943, he apparently had a change of heart, travelling down to San Francisco. FBI agents witnessed the reunion in a bar, Tatlock and Oppenheimer kissing on meeting. Later in the evening, they would go up to Tatlock's apartment, where Oppenheimer stayed all night. The next day, they went out for dinner before Oppenheimer left for the airport. Setting aside issues regarding the state of Oppenheimer's marriage, his assignation with Tatlock caused further security headaches. Given Tatlock's left-wing leanings and associations, Pash again recommended revoking Oppenheimer's security clearance, fearing that he was literally sleeping with the enemy. Groves and Lansdale disagreed, protecting their key asset and injecting realism into the paranoia.

Oppenheimer's relationship with Tatlock would terminate tragically. On 4 January 1943, she drowned herself in her bathtub in her apartment at 1405 Montgomery Street. Her father found her the next day, and through the tears of grief would read her short suicide note:

> I am disgusted with everything... To those who loved me and helped me, all love and courage. I wanted to live and to give and I got paralyzed somehow. I tried like hell to understand and couldn't... I think I would have been a liability all my life—at least I could take away the burden of a paralyzed soul from a fighting world.[70]

She said nothing of Oppenheimer, although it is recorded that her father destroyed a volume of her correspondence before the police arrived at the scene. Her note conveys a deeply troubled young woman wrestling with demons beyond anything the world could calm.

The government surveillance on Tatlock meant that the FBI was quickly informed of her suicide. That news was eventually passed to Oppenheimer via Peer de Silva, a station chief in the Central Intelligence Agency (CIA). Oppenheimer was distraught, Robert Serber observing that 'He was deeply grieved.'[71]

Tatlock's legacy may have been more than just the anguish and memories of family and friends. In 1962, Groves asked Oppenheimer directly why he called the very first atomic bomb 'Trinity'. He replied by saying that he had given the name in reference to some specific works of religious poetry by John Donne:

I did suggest it... Why I chose the name is not clear, but I know what thoughts were in my mind. There is a poem of John Donne, written just before his death, which I know and love. From it a quotation:

As West and East
In all flatt Maps—and I am one—are one,
So death doth touch the Resurrection.

In another, better known devotional poem Donne opens,

Batter my heart, three person'd God.[72]

Two specific Donne poems are quoted here: 'Hymn to God, My God, in My Sickness' and 'Batter my heart, three-person'd God', the latter a direct reference to the Christian doctrine of the Trinity. But it was Tatlock who had largely introduced Oppenheimer to the poetry of Donne. Maybe the searing fireball of the Trinity explosion in July 1945 gave, in Oppenheimer's mind, some form of brightly lit immortality to his former lover.

BUILDING A BOMB

It was not the bomb, it was the 'gadget'. In April 1943, Robert Serber gave a series of lectures to new arrivals at Los Alamos, which served as an 'indoctrination course' for those needing to get up to speed on the Manhattan Project. Condon subsequently wrote up these lectures and compiled them into a single document called the *Los Alamos Primer*. The opening statement from this document leaves the reader in no doubt about the purpose to which they were all now committed: 'The object of the project is to produce a practical military weapon in the form of a bomb in which the energy is released by a fast-neutron chain reaction in one or more of the materials known to show nuclear fission.'[73] Oppenheimer was present at the original lectures and decided that explicit terms referring to the bomb presented a security weakness. From now on, Serber should use the word 'gadget' – the catchy term stuck and became universal at Los Alamos.

The development of the gadget presented an unparalleled scientific and engineering challenge. Much of the detail regarding the theoretical and experimental work is beyond the scope of this book. But to comprehend just what Oppenheimer and his team achieved, and to give a framework for the subsequent narrative, it is useful to have a basic overview of how atomic and thermonu-clear bombs work. This is not just scientific context. The Manhattan Project was the beginning, not the end, of the nuclear-tipped Cold War, and the capabilities and possibilities of these devices would be at the centre of Oppenheimer's career for at least the next decade.

When talking of nuclear weapons we must distinguish between two types of device – atomic bombs and hydrogen bombs. Both of them work by releasing the energy contained in the nucleus of an atom, generating a destructive chain reaction, but at the atomic level they work in very different ways. The bombs developed for the attacks on Japan were atomic types working via the process of fission, splitting the atoms of two elements, uranium and plutonium. (Plutonium is present in nature, but in truly minute trace quantities, hence it is regarded as a man-made element, derived from uranium processing; this will have a significance to our evolving story.) As noted earlier, uranium has two isotopes: U-238 comprises the vast majority of the element, while U-235 constitutes only 0.7 per cent. Only U-235 is fissile – i.e. the nucleus is capable of being split by the impact of slow and fast neutrons. Under this impact, two or three free neutrons are released, striking other neutrons which in turn release free neutrons, and so on. The fission process releases quite enormous energy in the form of heat and gamma radiation. If this process is controlled, it provides productive atomic power; if it is uncontrolled, it is an atomic bomb. To ensure that a chain reaction is obtained, however, there needs to be enough of the element present to achieve 'critical mass', that is, the minimum amount of fissionable material that will ensure the chain reaction is self-sustaining. For U-235, the critical mass is around 47 kg (104 lb), although for practical purposes more is required, as the isotope is never pure. For Pu-239, the primary fissionable isotope of plutonium, the critical mass is around 10 kg (22 lb). During an atomic explosion, when the number of fission events increases with each generation of fission events, the bomb becomes 'super-critical' and will produce the explosive event.

Hydrogen bombs, also known as H-bombs or thermonuclear bombs, are the real monsters in the arsenal of nuclear weaponry, being orders of magnitude more powerful than atomic bombs. They work via the process of nuclear fusion rather than fission. When a hydrogen bomb is detonated, isotopes of hydrogen – specifically deuterium (which is naturally occurring) and tritium (which is artificially produced) – fuse into larger nuclei rather than split. To achieve this, an initial atomic explosion is required to provide the extreme temperatures and pressures necessary to overcome the electrostatic repulsion between the positively charged hydrogen nuclei. As the nuclei fuse, enormous energy is released because the mass of the resulting nucleus is less than the combined mass of the original nuclei, with the difference converted into energy according to Einstein's equation $E = mc^2$. The fused nuclei produce a stable helium nucleus and release fast neutrons. These fast neutrons can then induce fission reactions in the surrounding uranium or plutonium, which is used as a tamper material around the fusion reaction, further increasing the explosive yield. Both the fusion and the fission reactions are releasing enormous energy. Indeed, the explosive yield of the hydrogen is theoretically almost unlimited. This is why H-bomb effects are measured in equivalence to megatons of TNT, rather than the kilotons associated with A-bombs. H-bombs are true city-destroying devices.

In Los Alamos between 1943 and 1945, the primary focus of effort was on developing atomic weapons. But this did not mean that explorations of the H-bomb were completely overlooked. Back in July 1943 at Berkeley, Oppenheimer convened a meeting with a group of senior scientists, including Edward Teller (his presence in the H-bomb story will be paramount) to discuss the viability of the atomic bomb and also the theoretical possibility of building a hydrogen bomb, which they branded as the 'Super', a term simultaneously both ominous and jolly. The group soon concluded that the creation of a fission bomb was essentially a done deal – they were dramatically underestimating the complexities ahead of them – so turned to give the H-bomb their consideration. Their calculations of the power of the H-bomb were sobering, estimating that whereas 1 kg (2.2 lb) of uranium had the equivalence of 15,000–20,000 tons of TNT, a hydrogen bomb containing 1 kg of deuterium had the explosive force of 80,000–100,000 tons of TNT.

The H-bomb was a different animal altogether. In fact, during the discussions Teller raised the possibility that the H-bomb, and even possibly the A-bomb, might actually ignite the planet's atmosphere, with civilization-ending effects. Oppenheimer was naturally concerned about the possibility that their work was about to end life on Earth and ran the relevant calculations past other experts. He was eventually reassured on the point, but given the unprecedented nature of atomic weaponry there was always the haunting possibility of outcomes that no one could predict.

Subsequent explorations of H-bomb design were limited, but Oppenheimer permitted a small group at Los Alamos to keep investigating the theoretical basis of the design. This work would

Oppenheimer and Lawrence at the 184-inch cyclotron, University of California (Berkeley) Radiation Laboratory, c. 1946.

continue throughout the war years, even when it became clear that the magnitude of the scientific challenges meant that the H-bomb would not be viable in the immediate future. Oppenheimer appointed Teller to head the research group in June 1944, reporting to Oppenheimer once a week on progress. Thus work on the H-bomb ticked over in the background, but during the post-war years the Super would become the Holy Grail of nuclear weapon development. The pursuit of the Super would also drive a catastrophic wedge between Teller and Oppenheimer, resulting in Teller's effective destruction of Oppenheimer's reputation among the military-political establishment.

The scientific overview provided above contextualizes the immense scientific challenges faced by Oppenheimer and the Los Alamos team in developing just the A-bomb. The scientists had to push forward to new frontiers, well beyond existing knowledge, in domains such as physics, chemistry, metallurgy, engineering, ordnance design and logistics. Issues the Manhattan Project faced included the following:

- Moving from a theoretical understanding to the practical realization of the fission process, including how to initiate, control and sustain such a reaction.
- How to separate U-235 from U-238 (this process is known as 'enrichment') and how to manufacture plutonium, sufficient to gain enough of both materials to create a critical mass.
- Building the vast industrial infrastructure capable of uranium enrichment and plutonium purification at scale.
- Calculating the exact amount of materials necessary to achieve critical mass and the explosive yield that mass would produce, appropriate to the tactical and strategic objectives.
- Designing a device that could deliver the chain reaction in a controlled and precise manner at the exact moment; remember that an atomic explosion would result as soon as plutonium or uranium achieved a critical mass, whether intended or not.
- Turning the experimental and prototype models into a working bomb capable of being deployed by an existing type of military aircraft.
- Testing the device appropriately and safely – i.e. exploding an atomic bomb – within the confines of the continental USA.

This list was just the tip of a very large intellectual iceberg, each individual point branching out into great subsets of theoretical and intellectual challenges. Take, for example, the requirement to produce sufficient enriched uranium. In the early stages of the Manhattan Project, the focus was on centrifugal separation, but this proved unworkable. From December 1942, therefore, practical attention switched to two different methods: electromagnetic separation and gaseous diffusion. Both of these worked, but at output levels that were glacially slow. Scale was the compensation. Truly enormous uranium production plants were constructed at Oak Ridge: the 'Y-12' plant was dedicated to electromagnetic separation and the 'K-25' plant to gaseous diffusion. To give a sense of size and investment, note that by 1945 more than 22,000 people worked at Y-12 alone. Yet still progress was worryingly slow. In June 1944 the 'S-50' plant, working by the completely different method of liquid thermal diffusion, was brought online to increase the pace of fissionable uranium production.

To produce weapons-grade plutonium, by contrast, required the design, construction and operation of nuclear reactors; plutonium was a by-product of uranium used as reactor fuel. Three water-cooled nuclear reactors were built at the Hanford site by the chemicals giant DuPont, in addition to the 'X-10' separation plant, which performed the equally exacting work of separating plutonium from slugs of mixed radioactive materials. Cumulatively, getting enough suitable uranium and plutonium was a grinding headache for the Manhattan Project, a vast industry devoted to producing mere kilograms of usable material. By April 1945, for example, the Y-12 plant had produced only 25 kg (55 lb) of weapons-grade uranium and only enough for one 50 kg (110 lb) device by July 1945.

At every step of the way, Oppenheimer was the key facilitator helping to build bridges between scientific unknowns and practical weapons. Take the matter of bomb design. The laboratory work at Los Alamos was organized into four divisions: the Theoretical Division was led by Hans A. Bethe; Experimental Physics by Robert F. Bacher; Chemistry and Metallurgy by Joseph W. Kennedy; and Ordnance by US Navy captain and engineer William S. 'Deke' Parsons.

Parsons arrived at Los Alamos in May 1943. It was his job to turn the science into an actual working weapon, drawing upon his engineering and design experience in gunnery and explosives. Parsons concentrated his main effort on a 'gun-type' bomb design. In this design, the atomic weapon consists of two pieces of fissile uranium-235: a larger 'target' and a smaller 'bullet' of the same material. Individually, the two pieces were each of a sub-critical mass but would go super-critical when brought together. To unite the two, the target piece had a hollow section corresponding to the shape of the bullet. To achieve fission, the bullet was fired at very high speed into the target from a gun-type mechanism. At the moment the two pieces were united, critical mass was achieved, initiating the chain reaction and causing the explosion. The larger target piece was often surrounded by a tamper material to reflect escaping neutrons back into the fission process, maximizing the yield of the device and keeping the size of the weapon manageable.

The gun-type design was intended for application to both the uranium and the plutonium bombs. Two specific, sweetly named bombs were the goal: a U-235 device named 'Little Boy' and a Pu-239 gadget, 'Thin Man'. But while the gun-type uranium device was considered straightforward, so much so that pre-deployment testing was not required, the gun-type plutonium gadget resisted all efforts to make it work. Back in March 1943, Glenn T. Seaborg – a brilliant chemist who worked in the Chemistry and Metallurgy Division – discovered that Pu-239 also contained traces of the isotope Pu-240. The problem with this is that Pu-240 has a higher fission rate, which meant that as the two masses of plutonium were brought together they would fizzle and blow apart pre-emptively, reducing the energy available for the detonation of the bomb and causing malfunction or reduced yield. The specific engineering problem was that Parson's Ordnance Division could not develop a gun powerful enough (i.e. capable of delivering the required velocity) to prevent pre-detonation.

Thus, on 17 July 1944, Oppenheimer oversaw the difficult decision to cancel the gun-type plutonium bomb. There was another method of plutonium fission already in development, to which attention now turned. This was the implosion

Oppenheimer in 1944, only a year away from realizing a working atomic bomb.

method. The basic principle of implosion required that a sub-critical mass of plutonium be surrounded by a layer of high explosive. When the explosives were detonated, the inward force created would compress the plutonium into a super-critical state, initiating a nuclear chain reaction.

But achieving implosion was fiendishly complex. Indeed, Parsons regarded the precision required of the implosive force to be unachievable by conventional explosives. Oppenheimer had already authorized a small but important research group under Seth H. Neddermeyer, and this became the E-5 (Implosion) Group within the Ordnance Division. Oppenheimer's prescient advocacy of this group against much opposition would prove vital to the future of the Manhattan Project.

The progress of the implosion research was boosted by the input of the mathematician John von Neumann, who joined the project in September 1943 at Oppenheimer's insistence. Eventually the implosion team grew in size to 50 people, all heads down on the problem. Von Neumann, later assisted by the British physicist Rudolf E. Peierls, worked to improve the mathematical models of implosion. The team was also enhanced when Oppenheimer assigned Harvard chemist George B. Kistiakowsky, who was also Parson's deputy, to the implosion team, as a specialist in the engineering applications of explosives.

With the final decision to cancel the gun-type plutonium bomb, Oppenheimer knew he had to move fast to keep the project on its required trajectory. He undertook a major reorganization of the work at Los Alamos to ensure that implosion would become a viable solution. He assigned Robert Bacher to a new G [Gadget] Division, dedicated to the design and development of an implosion bomb, while Kistiakowsky headed X Division, which was focused on the conventional explosive components of the bomb. Parsons would, hopefully, bring all the parts together in a working device.

Through indefatigable effort, Kistiakowsky and his team, aided by the arrival in April 1944 of British scientist James Tuck, finally obtained the explosive geometric precision required for an effective implosion device. The solution lay in creating special shaped-charge 'explosive lenses' wrapped around the plutonium core, the explosive simultaneously delivering a uniform shockwave to take the core to criticality. The physics of making this work had been exhausting at an experimental level; the team conducted some 20,000 individual tests, the vast majority of them ending in misshapen lumps of metal that would indicate bomb failure in a working device. By March–April 1945, however, Oppenheimer had authorized and set the final design. Two bombs were now scheduled for production and deployment. 'Little Boy', the gun-type uranium design, was unchanged, but now it was accompanied by a plutonium implosion weapon called 'Fat Man', the name reflecting the rotund weapon profile necessitated by the implosion technology, as compared with the slimmer uranium device. (There was only enough uranium to make one gun-type uranium weapon, and the government knew they would need more than that. However, the gun-type plutonium design proved so troublesome that focus shifted to developing the plutonium implosion device.)

Unlike the uranium bomb, the implosion plutonium bomb would require a full atomic test before the USA took it to war. But the Manhattan Project was now nearly halfway through 1945, and thousands of American soldiers were still dying in the Pacific. Oppenheimer realized that a profound acceleration was required if the deadlines for a deliverable bomb were to be achieved – gadget testing was scheduled for July 1945 and a working device by 1 August.

By this time, much had changed politically and strategically, however. On 12 April 1945, President Roosevelt had died of a brain haemorrhage, to the shock of the American people and the US allies. Into his shoes stepped Harry S. Truman, a tough-minded Democrat keen to bring the war to a conclusion. The war with Germany ended soon after Truman's ascension – Adolf Hitler committed suicide on 30 April, and Germany signed a general unconditional surrender on 7 May. Well before Hitler killed himself, the Allies were aware that Germany was no longer practically in the race to build an atomic bomb. The German nuclear threat had been the original impetus for the Manhattan Project, so the fall of Hitler's Third Reich raised an existential question about the US project to build an atomic bomb. But the Allies were still at war with Japan. The horrors of the Pacific campaign meant that the US administration was now looking at the atomic bomb for its war-ending capabilities. The Japanese Pacific island of Iwo Jima, for example, was just 29.86 sq. km (11.53 sq. miles) in area, but the battle to clear it between 9 February and 26 March 1945 resulted in 19,000 Japanese dead, 6,800 American dead and more than 17,000 American wounded. The almost non-existent numbers of Japanese wounded were the result of the Japanese defenders choosing to fight to the death rather than surrender. The even larger Battle of Okinawa on 1 April–22 June 1945 produced total casualties on both sides of c.180,000. Such terrifying numbers, and the suicidal Japanese defence, made US planners fearful of the cost of taking the Japanese home islands, and here the atomic bombs offered a possible shortcut to victory. Furthermore, a demonstration of unilateral atomic capability could humble the Soviet Union, which was already emerging as an ideological threat to the post-war European political order.

SEEING IT THROUGH

The changes in the international strategic situation might have given Oppenheimer pause for thought about the relevance and purpose of the bomb he was guiding to fruition. But based on his moral investment in the Manhattan Project, and his clear understanding of atomic bomb effects, we cannot make this conclusion. Certainly, Oppenheimer was perfectly aware of the terrifying destructive force of an atomic bomb when unleashed on an urban ground target. Back in a conference in April 1943, Oppenheimer summed up the 'Present Knowledge' to the gathered scientists:

> Energy Release: The destructive effect of the gadget is due to radiative effects and the shock wave generated by the explosion. The shock wave effect seems to extend over the biggest area and would be, therefore, most important. The area devastated by the shock wave is proportional to the 2/3 power of the energy release and may be simply calculated by comparing the energy release with that of TNT. If the reaction would go to completion, then 50 kg of 25 would be equivalent to 10 tons of TNT. Actually it is very difficult to obtain a large percentage of the potential energy release.[74]

Of course, at this stage the bomb was still highly theoretical. Certainly, Oppenheimer's misgivings about the national strategic application of the atomic bomb would grow over time. But by May 1945, he was nevertheless an active participant in the 'Target Committee', the mixed group of military and scientific personnel whose collective purpose was to decide upon when, where and how the bomb was to be dropped. Unclassified notes of the meetings reveal the members of the group, including Oppenheimer, fine-tuning the proposed attacks on Japan, and moral wranglings are nowhere to be seen. From Committee meetings on 10–11 May, the first page of the minutes laid out the agenda:

> 2. The agenda for the meetings presented by Dr. Oppenheimer consisted of the following:

> A.   Height of Detonation

B.   Report on Weather and Operations

C.   Gadget Jettisoning and Landing

D.   Status of Targets

E.   Psychological Factors in Target Selection

F.   Use Against Military Objectives

G.   Radiological Effects

H.   Coordinated Air Operations[75]

The minutes go on to show that by May 1945 five specific targets in Japan had been selected: Kyoto, Hiroshima, Yokohama, Kokura Arsenal and Niigata. In July 1945, however, the US Secretary of War Henry L. Stimson had persuaded the President to remove Kyoto from the list, Stimson feeling squeamish about erasing such a radiant cultural centre. (Stimson had actually visited Kyoto on several occasions during the 1920s in his role as governor of the Philippines.) Nagasaki took its place.

Oppenheimer's views on the targeting are not recorded, and likely weren't solicited, but there are other points in the minutes where he is mentioned specifically, again showing that he was under no illusions about what they were about to unleash on the world:

9. Radiological Effect

A.   Dr. Oppenheimer presented a memo he had prepared on the radiological effects of the gadget. This memo will not be repeated in this summary but is being sent to General Groves as a separate exhibit. The basic recommendations of this memo are (1) for radiological reasons no aircraft should be closer than 2-1/2 miles to the point of detonation (for blast reasons the distance should be greater) and (2) aircraft must avoid the cloud of radio-active materials. If other aircraft are to conduct missions shortly after the detonation a monitoring plane should determine the areas to be avoided.[76]

So, Oppenheimer was fully committed to the practical delivery of an atomic bomb in a heavily populated target. But at the same time, he was looking ahead to the future, and here we find more ambiguity creeping in. Oppenheimer, Compton, Fermi and Lawrence had been appointed to the Scientific Advisory Panel of the War Department's Interim Committee, formed in May 1945 to develop policy recommendations for the post-war applications of atomic energy and weaponry. In the minutes of a meeting held on 31 May 1945, Oppenheimer introduced a personal vision of international atomic collaboration:

> It might be wise for the United States to offer to the world free interchange of information with particular emphasis on the development of peace-time uses. The basic goal of all endeavors in the field should be the enlargement of human welfare. If we were to offer to exchange information before the bomb was actually used, our moral position would be greatly strengthened.[77]

The overall thrust of this statement is critical to understanding Oppenheimer's roller-coaster political experience after 1945. He, like many others, was dismayed not so much by the development of atomic weaponry (although there were certainly those who did protest), nor in its intended use to end the Second World War, but rather in the way that the USA was keeping its nuclear knowledge so close to its chest, rather than sharing it with its allies. Many within the Manhattan Project saw this policy stance as propagating a disastrous future arms race, one that now had apocalyptic, city-destroying tools in the opposing forces. The US scientists working on the Manhattan Project had no doubt that the Soviets would ultimately work out how to build atomic weapons. Many in the US government, however, including President Truman, arrogantly dismissed Soviet intellect out of hand, seeing the necessary science and engineering as forever beyond Soviet reach.

The position of Oppenheimer and many other Los Alamos scientists became more developed in a meeting in June 1945. I here quote it at length because of its importance as a framework for understanding Oppenheimer's post-war struggles:

You have asked us to comment on the initial use of the new weapon. This use, in our opinion, should be such as to promote a satisfactory adjustment of our international relations. At the same time, we recognize our obligation to our nation to use the weapons to help save American lives in the Japanese war.

(1) To accomplish these ends we recommend that before the weapons are used not only Britain, but also Russia, France, and China be advised that we have made considerable progress in our work on atomic weapons, that these may be ready to use during the present war, and that we would welcome suggestions as to how we can cooperate in making this development contribute to improved international relations.

(2) The opinions of our scientific colleagues on the initial use of these weapons are not unanimous: they range from the proposal

of a purely technical demonstration to that of the military application best designed to induce surrender. Those who advocate a purely technical demonstration would wish to outlaw the use of atomic weapons, and have feared that if we use the weapons now our position in future negotiations will be prejudiced. Others emphasize the opportunity of saving American lives by immediate military use, and believe that such use will improve the international prospects, in that they are more concerned with the prevention of war than with the elimination of this specific weapon. We find ourselves closer to these latter views; we can propose no technical demonstration likely to bring an end to the war; we see no acceptable alternative to direct military use.

(3) With regard to these general aspects of the use of atomic energy, it is clear that we, as scientific men, have no proprietary rights. It is true that we are among the few citizens who have had occasion to give thoughtful consideration to these problems during the past few years. We have, however, no claim to special competence in solving the political, social, and military problems which are presented by the advent of atomic power.[78]

A key phrase in this text is surely 'we see no acceptable alternative to direct military use'. Oppenheimer had done his soul-searching, but the cruel truths of war meant that he and many others saw the only way to end the conflict was terrible kinetics. Regarding the big picture of international order, Oppenheimer urges the sharing of information with key allies, including Russia, to lay the foundation for long-term understanding and strategic order. The humility of his statement in paragraph (3) can be read against his latent concern that the supreme powers were ignoring or mishandling questions of supreme importance to global humanity.

Big-picture aside, the fact was that Oppenheimer and the team needed to press the accelerator hard to the floor if they were to be ready to drop the bomb. Much of the work of 1945 was conducted under a troubled atmosphere. Morale was low among many of the scientists, worn down by intellectual effort and constant setbacks. Oppenheimer and Groves faced very real problems in getting enough scientists, engineers, logisticians and other key workers to give the project its final surge to conclusion. Oppenheimer, Groves and Conant collectively galvanized the final push, pumping in materiel and personnel from wherever it could be sourced. For a key date was now set in the schedule – the first explosion of an atomic bomb on the face of the earth. That bomb would be Trinity.

Los Alamos became a strange, enclosed world for many of the world's greatest scientists. Here Oppenheimer socializes, c. 1945.

TRINITY, LITTLE BOY AND FAT MAN

The preparation and planning for the test explosion of Trinity had begun back in 1944, under the direction of Harvard physicist Kenneth Bainbridge. An immediate priority was to find a site in which the gadget could be tested – by which we mean exploded – safely and securely. Bainbridge found that location again in New Mexico, in a remote and flat desert region known colloquially, and appropriately, as the *Jornada del Muerto* ('Journey of Death'), some 338 km (210 miles) from Los Alamos. It was already, conveniently, a militarized area, being inside the Alamogordo Bombing and Gunnery Range (renamed the White Sands Proving Ground on 9 July 1945) of Alamogordo Air Base. Oppenheimer and Groves approved the location in the autumn of 1944.

The test explosion was scheduled for 16 July 1945. Months of round-the-clock preparation lay ahead, not only in designing and readying the bomb itself, but also in installing infrastructure, protective bunkers, accommodation, measuring instruments, communication trenches, signal networks and much more. To gain a partial sense of what they might be dealing with in July, the bomb team conducted a test detonation of 100 tons of TNT on 7 May, a blast event that revealed the need for major improvements in monitoring and data-gathering systems for the atomic explosion.

The final Trinity device scarcely resembled a bomb. Unlike the final devices, which were configured to be dropped from an aircraft and had a recognizable bomb configuration, Trinity was rather a great misshapen sphere designed for static detonation, wrapped in snaking cables. To simulate an airburst explosion, on 14 July the gadget was hoisted atop a 30 m (100 ft)-high steel tower in

The 'Trinity' explosion at Los Alamos, Alamogordo, New Mexico , 16 July 1945..

the centre of the test area. Stormy weather passed over the site in the immediate hours before the explosion, raising concern at some points that lightning might actually trigger an atomic explosion.

People now began to gather for the final test, more than 450 in total, including Oppenheimer and many of the world's top scientists and military leaders. Some of the scientists were placing wagers, comparing their predictions of the actual explosive yield. All wanted to see how millions of lines of scientific theory, millions of work-hours of labour, would translate into physical reality. To establish points from which the blast could be observed, engineer teams had built a series of shelters around the test site, at a distance of 9,100 m (10,000 yards) from the epicentre. All the personnel had been given welding goggles to shield their eyes from the initial blinding flash; they were told to lie down with their backs to the blast, only to stand up and turn around when the initial explosion had subsided.

For Oppenheimer, occupying the protective shelter 'South 10,000' with Groves and other senior personnel, the countdown to detonation was an agony of dilated time. Career-ending failure was a possibility. But there was also the heart-thumping expectation, the anticipation for an event of celestial grandeur, conducted on a flat plain of earth in New Mexico.

Finally, at 05.29.45 on 16 July 1945, Trinity unleashed itself. Brigadier General Thomas F. Farrell, one of the individuals who shared the shelter with Oppenheimer, later painted the scene of what must have been a near-religious experience for Oppenheimer:

In that brief instant in the remote New Mexico desert the tremendous effort of the brains and brawn of all these people came suddenly and startlingly to the fullest fruition. Dr. Oppenheimer, on whom had rested a very heavy burden, grew tenser as the last seconds ticked off. He scarcely breathed. He held on to a post to steady himself. For the last few seconds, he stared directly ahead and then when the announcer shouted 'Now!' and there came this tremendous burst of light followed shortly thereafter by the deep growling roar of the explosion, his face relaxed into an expression of tremendous relief. Several of the observers standing back of the shelter to watch the lighting effects were knocked flat by the blast.

The tension in the room let up and all started congratulating each other. Everyone sensed 'This is it!' No matter what might happen now all knew that the impossible scientific job had been done. Atomic fission would no longer be hidden in the cloisters of the theoretical physicists' dreams. It was almost full grown at birth. It was a great new force to be used for good or for evil. There was a feeling in that shelter that those concerned with its nativity should dedicate their lives to the mission that it would always be used for good and never for evil.

Dr. Kistiakowsky, the impulsive Russian, threw his arms around Dr. Oppenheimer and embraced him with shouts of glee. Others were equally enthusiastic. All the pent-up emotions were released in those few minutes and all seemed to sense immediately that the explosion had far exceeded the most optimistic expectations and wildest hopes of the scientists. All seemed to feel that they had been present at the birth of a new age—The Age of Atomic Energy—and felt their profound responsibility to help in guiding into right

Oppenheimer (left) and General Leslie Groves (right) inspect the aftermath of the Trinity test at Ground Zero; they are stood in front of the remains of one leg of the test tower..

channels the tremendous forces which had been unlocked for the first time in history.[79]

Farrell captured an important truth – after 16 July 1945, the world would never be the same again. Groves himself described the explosion with rather more surgical phrasing, but the magnitude of what had been witnessed, and what destruction could be unleashed, remained clear:

3. The test was successful beyond the most optimistic expecta-

tions of anyone. Based on the data which it has been possible to work up to date, I estimate the energy generated to be in excess of the equivalent of 15,000 to 20,000 tons of TNT; and this is a conservative estimate. Data based on measurements which we have not yet been able to reconcile would make the energy release several times the conservative figure. There were tremendous blast effects. For a brief period there was a lighting effect within a radius of 20 miles equal to several suns in midday; a huge ball of fire was formed which lasted for several seconds. This ball mushroomed and rose to a height of over ten thousand feet before it dimmed. The light from the explosion was seen clearly at Albuquerque, Santa Fe, Silver City, El Paso and other points generally to about 180 miles away. The sound was heard to the same distance in a few instances but generally to about 100 miles. Only a few windows were broken although one was some 125 miles away. A massive cloud was formed which surged and billowed upward with tremendous power, reaching the substratosphere at an elevation of 41,000 feet, 36,000 feet above the ground, in about five minutes, breaking without interruption through a temperature inversion at 17,000 feet which most of the scientists thought would stop it. Two supplementary explosions occurred in the cloud shortly after the main explosion. The cloud contained several thousand tons of dust picked up from the ground and a considerable amount of iron in the gaseous form. Our present thought is that this iron ignited when it mixed with the oxygen in the air to cause these supplementary explosions. Huge concentrations of highly radioactive materials resulted from the fission and were contained in this cloud.

4. A crater from which all vegetation had vanished, with a diameter of 1200 feet and a slight slope toward the center, was formed. In the center was a shallow bowl 130 feet in diameter and 6 feet in depth. The material within the crater was deeply pulverised dirt. The material within the outer circle is greenish and can be distinctly seen from as much as 5 miles away. The steel from the tower was evaporated. 1500 feet away there was a four-inch iron pipe 16 feet high set in concrete and strongly guyed. It disappeared completely.[80]

But beyond such voices, it was surely Oppenheimer who captured the spirit of the experience better than anyone else. In a 1965 television documentary, he remembered the Trinity explosion as a transformation in the relation of self to the world:

We knew the world would not be the same. A few people laughed, a few people cried. Most people were silent. I remembered the line from the Hindu scripture, the *Bhagavad Gita*; Vishnu is trying to persuade the Prince that he should do his duty and, to impress him, takes on his multi-armed form and says, 'Now I am become Death, the destroyer of worlds.'[81]

The footage of this interview is haunting to watch. We see a man lost in memories, capturing the numinous gravity of a portentous moment in human history. The Manhattan Project, and Oppenheimer, had achieved what they had set out to do.

The subsequent history is familiar, but still sobering. On 6 and 9 August 1945, the cities of Hiroshima and Nagasaki respectively were seared from the face of the earth by two atomic bombs, delivered by US Army Air Force (USAAF) B-29 Superfortress bombers. Estimates of how many human beings died in these two events are clouded by the impossibility of accurate assessments under such chaotic, apocalyptic conditions. Certainly, many tens of thousands of people died in the sun-intensity heat and flame given off by the initial blast, and from the super-charged blast winds. By the time radiation had worked its effects among the ruins and the survivors over the next four months, as many as 226,000 people may have died.

At Los Alamos, the initial news of the successful Hiroshima bombing released euphoric emotions. Oppenheimer was at the heart of the celebrants. Others found quiet corners to shudder at the thought of what they had unleashed. Now Oppenheimer had to live with the consequences. Arguably his greatest challenges were still to come.

CHAPTER 5

FALLOUT

The global conflagration that was the Second World War mercifully ended on 2 September 1945. High-ranking government and military delegations, representing both the victorious and the vanquished, clustered aboard the deck of the American battleship USS *Missouri*, anchored in Tokyo Bay, to witness the formal signing of the Japanese surrender.

The role of the atomic bombs in bringing about that final capitulation has been debated by historians ever since. Were they the decisive instrument, or should they be contextually downgraded by the city-erasing conventional bombing campaign that was already in full swing? Was it rather the Soviet invasion of Manchuria on 9 August 1945 that tipped the balance? Was Japan preparing to surrender anyway, even prior to the Hiroshima bomb? Regardless of the discussions between historical schools of thought, the atomic bombs were clearly, devastatingly, instrumental in the final act of surrender, even if they were only one among many powerful causes. But for the victors, the debate that ensued was not over the final end of hostilities. Rather, the key question was now, What next for atomic power? That question generated intense heat and light in the immediate post-war years and defined the direction of the emerging Cold War. It would also dominate Oppenheimer's life for the next decade, nearly destroying him in the process.

Top: This photograph taken in early 1946 shows (left to right): Dr. Ernest O. Lawrence, Director of the University of California Radiation Laboratory, Dr. Glenn T. Seaborg, head of the Chemistry Division of the Laboratory, and Dr. J. Robert Oppenheimer.

Above: Oppenheimer (second row, centre) participates in the 1946 colloquium on the 'Super' bomb at Los Alamos. Already, the disagreements over the future of nuclear weapon development were becoming bitter.

NEW WORLD ORDER

Months before the Japanese surrender, Oppenheimer was already wrestling with the official American position on the atomic future. The nuclear genie was out of the bottle. How would the world manage the weapons technology, existing and new devices (and the stockpiles they would create), and fissile material production facilities? More advanced bombs and delivery systems would surely come, as would the inevitability that countries other than the USA would master atomic weaponry. How could the planet prevent a terrifying nuclear arms race, which at its theoretical extreme was surely a negative-sum game?

After the mushroom clouds dissipated over Hiroshima and Nagasaki, and the effects of the bombs became visible, Oppenheimer developed grave doubts about the human capacity to manage them. His mounting anxiety was compounded by deepening insight into the empirical consequences of atomic weaponry. As the days and weeks went on, an increasing volume of military reports and press articles were published about the atomic bombings, including first-hand accounts from survivors and aftermath reporting from journalists on the scene. The horrors they witnessed were disturbing to read, a grotesque litany of twisted steel and smashed concrete, humans reduced to ash, slow death from radiation sickness. Oppenheimer was particularly unsettled by the dropping of the second bomb on Nagasaki, seeing it more as chest-thumping political and military excess rather than a military necessity. An FBI report of this time described Oppenheimer as a 'nervous wreck', such was his emotional turmoil.[82]

Just eight days after the attack on Nagasaki, Oppenheimer sent a letter to Stimson under the remit of the Interim Committee. Here quoted in full, it spelled out Oppenheimer's early concerns about government policy in relation to the atomic weapons:

From: J R Oppenheimer

To: Henry Stimson, Secretary of War

Date: August 17, 1945

Dear Mr. Secretary:

The Interim Committee has asked us to report in some detail on the scope and program of future work in the field of atomic energy. One important phase of this work is the development of weapons; and since this is the problem which has dominated our war time activities, it is natural that in this field our ideas should be most definite and clear, and that we should be most confident of answering adequately the questions put to us by the committee. In examining these questions we have, however, come on certain quite general conclusions, whose implications for national policy would seem to be both more immediate and more profound than those of the detailed technical recommendations to be submitted. We, therefore, think it appropriate to present them to you at this time.

1. We are convinced that weapons quantitatively and qualitatively far more effective than now available will result from further work on these problems. This conviction is motivated not alone by analogy with past developments, but by specific projects to improve

and multiply the existing weapons, and by the quite favorable technical prospects of the realization of the super bomb.

2. We have been unable to devise or propose effective military counter-measures for atomic weapons. Although we realize that future work may reveal possibilities at present obscure to us, it is our firm opinion that no military countermeasures will be found which will be adequately effective in preventing the delivery of atomic weapons.

The detailed technical report in preparation will document these conclusions, but hardly alter them.

3. We are not only unable to outline a program that would assure to this nation for the next decades hegemony in the field of atomic weapons; we are equally unable to insure that such hegemony, if achieved, could protect us from the most terrible destruction.

4. The development, in the years to come, of more effective atomic weapons, would appear to be a most natural element in any national policy of maintaining our military forces at great strength; nevertheless we have grave doubts that this further development can contribute essentially or permanently to the prevention of war. We believe that the safety of this nation – as opposed to its ability to inflict damage on an enemy power – cannot lie wholly or even primarily in its scientific or technical prowess. It can be based only on making future wars impossible. It is our unanimous and urgent recommendation to you that, despite the present incomplete exploitation of technical possibilities in this field, all steps be

taken, all necessary international arrangements be made, to this one end.

5. We should be most happy to have you bring these views to the attention of other members of the Government, or of the American people, should you wish to do so.

Very sincerely,
J. R. Oppenheimer[83]

Clearly, Oppenheimer felt there was an urgent need for the US government to make a policy clarification about how it would handle its new, God-like destructive power.

Clause 4 in particular reflected Oppenheimer's endorsement of the strategic position outlined by Niels Bohr. Bohr was an open advocate for international co-operation regarding the science, technology and resources of atomic weaponry. He argued that the collaborative position should be extended to the Soviets. Indeed, he saw that as essential to guarantee future world peace. His arguments, which he was able to present personally to both Truman and Churchill, fell on deaf ears at the government level. Rather, he seems merely to have heightened the suspicions (unfounded) that he was a Soviet spy. His policy outlook, however, was prevalent among many of the scientists of Los Alamos. In fact, in August 1945 a sizeable group of those scientists formed the Association of Los Alamos Scientists (ALAS). The contrite acronym says much about their position. Like Bohr, they began campaigning for the internationalist position.

Oppenheimer also could no longer take the path of least resistance. In addition to the letter he personally handed to Stimson, he also signed and sent a policy document drafted by ALAS. One of its central arguments to the US administration was that regardless of security efforts, the science and technology of atomic weaponry were not prohibitive barriers to other countries developing such weapons. No matter what the USA did, other nations – including the Soviet Union – would eventually have the bomb. That would lead to an arms race and potential nuclear war, unless the world could establish a co-operative framework.

But over the subsequent months, instead of exploring constructive openness, the US administration simply held its nuclear cards even closer to its chest. Nor was this just a game of intellectual property. The relationship between the USA and the Soviet Union was deteriorating fast in the political and ideological carve-up of post-war Europe and Asia, even threatening a new international conflict. So the flame of co-operation was already flickering out. Emerging policy developments simply widened the fractures and encouraged growing dissent within the USA.

A key sticking point was the May–Johnson Bill, a policy framework sent to Congress by the Truman administration on 3 October 1945. In summary, the bill advocated for the establishment of an Atomic Energy Commission (AEC) to oversee all aspects of post-war nuclear policy, both civilian and military. As conceived, the AEC would consist of nine commissioners appointed by the President, with the balance of members weighted towards military authority. In addition, the bill made it clear that the USA's hard-won understanding of practical nuclear weaponry would not be shared internationally. In fact, there would be grave penalties for transferring secrets beyond the USA or its approved strategic partners.

Despite his internationalist mindset, Oppenheimer supported the May–Johnson Bill, giving testimony on its behalf in Congress. Such was his authority and persuasion at Los Alamos, he even brought ALAS on to the side of the bill. But there were many other scientists working in Chicago, Oak Ridge and also at Los Alamos who united in vigorous opposition, and ultimately their opposition killed the bill's progression through Congress. A major bone of contention was whether a military or civilian body had supreme control over atomic energy and strategy. Thus on 20 December, an alternative bill was put forward by Democratic Senator Brien McMahon. This bill proposed nuclear governance by a purely civilian body of five commissioners, again presidential appointees, who would take control not only of the production of fissionable materials, but also over the construction and the stockpiling of nuclear weaponry.

The McMahon Bill, as it was known, was signed into law on 1 August 1946 as part of the new Atomic Energy Act (AEA), although by the time it hit the statute books major revisions meant that the military and the President still had a significant controlling influence over decision-making, especially when acting in the interests of national defence. The Act established some other oversight bodies that would have a significant impact upon Oppenheimer's future. The nine-person General Advisory Committee (GAC) was purposed to feed policy guidance to the AEC on scientific and technical matters, while the Military Liaison Committee (MLC) was to give the perspective from the senior defence leadership. The Act also established a Joint Committee on Atomic Energy (JCAE) from members of the Senate and the House of Representatives to provide political and legislative frameworks on nuclear policy.

Oppenheimer was appointed to the GAC on 10 December 1946. The fact that each person on the committee was approved by the President illustrates the extent to which Oppenheimer was seen politically as a safe pair of hands by the administration. But in reality, Oppenheimer was deeply conflicted. Back on 25 October 1945, Oppenheimer had been granted a one-to-one meeting with Truman, after some weeks of stubborn pushing for a presidential audience. The fact that Oppenheimer was granted access to the Oval Office says much about his status at that time. He was already something of a celebrity among officialdom and the general public. Job offers of every hue – academic, commercial and governmental – poured in, most of which he deflected or ignored. Oppenheimer later accepted that he had attained a social status rare for a scientist – that of being famous – and he also reflected on the epithet that still attaches to his name: 'I had become widely regarded as a principle author or inventor of the atomic bomb, more widely, I well knew, than the facts warranted. In a modest way I had become a kind of public personage. I was deluged, as I have been ever since, with requests to lecture and to take part in numerous scientific activities and public affairs. Most of these I did not accept.'[84]

Oppenheimer might well have been known as the 'Father of the Atomic Bomb', but in the meeting with Truman any position or attitude of superiority was not apparent. To Oppenheimer's dismay, his internationalist position was countered by Truman's possessive secrecy regarding atomic weaponry, and the belief that the general backwardness of the Soviet people would prevent them from ever developing a bomb of their own. Oppenheimer, thrown by the obdurate position of his President, became bumbling and hesitant, so much so that Truman actually asked him what the matter was. Famously, he replied, 'Mr President, I feel that I have blood on my hands.' Clearly, Oppenheimer was wrestling with the moral consequences of what the Manhattan Project had achieved, under his leadership. But the anguish simply angered Truman. One account has Truman giving Oppenheimer his handkerchief and sarcastically saying, 'Well, here, would you like to wipe your hands?' Certainly, Truman later told prominent public attorney and public administrator David Lilienthal, 'I told him the blood was on my hands—to let me worry about that,' and also referred to him as a 'cry-baby'.[85]

Arguments about whether Oppenheimer came to regret his work on the Manhattan Project have been central to the evolving biographical portrait of this complex man. To clarify, it is worth comparing his one-line mea culpa delivered to Truman with other statements around this time. On 16 October 1945 Oppenheimer had resigned his directorship of Los Alamos, thereby giving his public voice a little more freedom. On 2 November, Oppenheimer gave a speech to ALAS, in which he reflected on the scientific position and on the concerns of ALAS members:

> But when you come right down to it the reason that we did this job is because it was an organic necessity. If you are a scientist you cannot stop such a thing. If you are a scientist you believe that it is good to find out how the world works; that it is good to find out what the realities are; that it is good to turn over to mankind at large the greatest possible power to control the world and to deal with it according to its lights and its values.
> [...]

But what is surely the thing which must have troubled you, and which troubled me, in the official statements was the insistent note of unilateral responsibility for the handling of atomic weapons. However good the motives of this country are—I am not going to argue with the President's description of what the motives and the aims are—we are 140 million people, and there are two billion people living on earth. We must understand that whatever our commitments to our own views and ideas, and however confident we are that in the course of time they will tend to prevail, our absolute—our completely absolute—commitment to them, in denial of the views and ideas of other people, cannot be the basis of any kind of agreement.[86]

One of the most striking elements of this passage is Oppenheimer's argument regarding 'organic necessity'. Oppenheimer offers science as a compulsion, the requirement to unmask physical reality regardless of where that leads. Note, however, that he is not admitting moral blindness, but rather an obligation scientists have to pursue truth and insight when the requirement is identified. But in the second paragraph here, Oppenheimer switches the focus specifically to the outcome, atomic weapons. In beautifully crafted phrases, Oppenheimer reiterates the internationalist argument, namely, that the power to destroy all mankind must be owned by all if it is to be annulled. He acknowledges that he and his audience are 'troubled' by the current state of policy, accentuated by the hint of sarcasm when referring to the President's 'motives' and 'aims'.

Another frame of comparison is provided by a speech Oppenheimer gave on 16 November 1945, upon receipt of the Army-Navy 'Excellence' Award:

It is with appreciation and gratefulness that I accept from you this scroll for the Los Alamos Laboratory, and for the men and women whose work and whose hearts have made it. It is our hope that in years to come we may look at the scroll and all that it signifies, with pride.

Today that pride must be tempered by a profound concern. If atomic bombs are to be added as new weapons to the arsenals of a warring world, or to the arsenals of the nations preparing for war, then the time will come when mankind will curse the names of Los Alamos and Hiroshima.

The people of this world must unite or they will perish. This war, that has ravaged so much of the earth, has written these words. The atomic bomb has spelled them out for all men to understand. Other men have spoken them in other times, and of other wars, of other weapons. They have not prevailed. There are some misled by a false sense of human history, who hold that they will not prevail today.

It is not for us to believe that. By our minds we are committed, committed to a world united, before the common peril, in law and in humanity.[87]

The first paragraph quoted here is nuanced. He sees that the work at Los Alamos should be regarded rightly with pride, implying that there is nothing inherently shameful about the scientific efforts of the scientists and engineers. But it is a pride somewhat held in abeyance, waiting until history reveals its outcomes. 'Unite or perish' is, ultimately, Oppenheimer's overriding message.

In the first 18 months following the atomic bombings on Japan, Oppenheimer was acting within a window of opportunity to influence nascent nuclear policy. At the beginning of 1946, he was appointed to the Board of Consultants serving a Presidential Review Commission, chaired by the Under Secretary of State Dean Acheson, working alongside David Lilienthal and other informed figures. The Board was tasked with producing a report outlining the specific possibilities for the international control of nuclear weapons. Not unexpectedly, Oppenheimer had already formulated the outline of such

Oppenheimer appears before the Senate Atomic Energy Committee in Washington DC on 5 December 1945; acting as a scientific advisor, his opinions were not always to the liking of the Committee.

Oppenheimer at the Guest Lodge in Oak Ridge, c. February 1946.

a plan, collaborating with fellow internationalist Isidor Rabi. Oppenheimer took the ideas forward into the final *Report on the International Control of Atomic Energy*, aka the 'Acheson–Lilienthal Plan'. (Despite the shortened name, the plan was largely based upon a memo Oppenheimer sent to Lilienthal.)

Note that this was not a confidential work – it was actually published for public consumption, at the price of 35 cents – and it had no statutory force. Among its many pages, it made a clear recommendation:

Summary of Proposed Plan The proposal contemplates an international agency conducting all intrinsically dangerous operations in the nuclear field, with individual nations and their citizens free to conduct, under license and a minimum of inspection, all non-dangerous, or safe, operations.

The international agency might take any one of several forms, as a UNO Commission, or an international corporation or authority. We shall refer to it as Atomic Development Authority [ADA]. It must have authority to own and lease property; and to carry on mining, manufacturing, research, licensing, inspecting, selling, or any other necessary operations.[88]

This was radical stuff. Under the structural proposition, the ADA would control all of the world's fissile and fissionable materials, hence no single nation would be able to build bombs unilaterally (including the USA).

The erratic forward bounce of history would reshape the Acheson–Lilienthal Plan. As ideological and strategic tensions increased between the West and the Soviet Union, on 5 March 1946 Winston Churchill gave his impactful 'Iron Curtain' speech at Fulton, Missouri, part of which included the explicit caution against sharing nuclear knowledge. Thus the Acheson–Lilienthal Plan was heavily reworked for the US administration by Bernard Baruch, the US representative to the United Nations Atomic Energy Commission. By the time the 'Baruch Plan' arrived at the UN in June 1946, it retained vestiges of international control of nuclear weapons, alongside crucial changes. Responsible only to the UN Security Council (UNSC), an Atomic Development Authority would have an international oversight and inspection role, including the power to seize facilities at which illegal (i.e. unauthorized) atomic bombs were being developed. But at the same time, the plan removed veto power from UNSC members against any nation conducting prohibited activities. The United Nations would only begin destroying its nuclear arsenal once the plan was implemented.[89]

The Baruch Plan proved unacceptable to the Soviets. Not only would it mean that they had to relinquish veto power over atomic matters on the UNSC, but it would also give the West inspection rights over Soviet atomic organizations, plus it would enable the USA, for now, to retain its fledgling nuclear arsenal. The discussions within the UN ground to a halt, and the suspicions between East and West only intensified.

FALLOUT

Oppenheimer's plan for an internationalist approach to nuclear policy was fading fast. Another nail in its coffin came in July 1946, when the USA conducted its first atomic bomb tests since Trinity. Plans for these tests, what would become known as Operation Crossroads, were first announced by Admiral William Blandy to the President's Evaluation Commission, which included Oppenheimer, on 30 March 1946. Blandy was to head Joint Task Force One, the team responsible for test design and implementation. In significant contrast to Trinity, Crossroads was to be conducted over the remote Bikini Atoll in the Pacific Marshall Islands, specifically to test the effects of atomic explosions against warships (surplus Allied and former Axis vessels). The test would detonate two separate bombs, one an above-water explosion and the other an underwater shot.

The proposal saw quite some pushback from the scientific community, including Oppenheimer, who posited that the data they hoped to glean from the tests could be derived from modelling rather than the inflammatory act of actual explosions. Oppenheimer grew more convinced of his position, and on 3 May sent a personal letter to the President outlining his objections. He not only questioned the analytical value of the tests, especially given the costs to the taxpayer, but he also raised some strategic considerations:

3. It has been suggested that we must be prepared for the possibility of atomic warfare, and must take the necessary steps in our own defense. Surely the overwhelming effectiveness of atomic weapons lies in their use for the bombardment of cities, and of centers of production and population. The problems involved in preparation

for these dangers are indeed, should we face them, most difficult. Much study and a vast effort would be required. In comparison with these issues, the detailed determination of the destructiveness of atomic weapons against naval craft would appear trivial.[90]

This is an interesting position statement. Having shown some squeamishness about the destructive consequences of atomic weaponry, here Oppenheimer is trying to direct Truman's attention *towards* the city-destroying capabilities of the devices as strategic tools. The tactical application of atomic weapons against shipping he regards as 'trivial'. What is notable about this statement is that over subsequent years his position would shift, particularly relating to the applications of the hydrogen bomb. In that context, Oppenheimer was keen to focus thinking more towards localized tactical applications of nuclear weaponry rather than widespread area destruction. We do not have to see this as confused thinking or even hypocrisy. Oppenheimer was at the centre of unprecedented historical changes in military technology and international relations. Like many in similar positions, Oppenheimer was working out his position in real time.

Oppenheimer's protests against Operation Crossroads fell on deaf ears. The two atomic weapons – codenamed 'Able' and 'Baker' – erupted over the Pacific in July 1946, delivering both devastation and data to a military establishment keen to consolidate its lead over the Soviets. The active testing of nuclear weapons would thereafter become a habit the USA, and later the Soviet Union and nuclear-tipped US allies, would find hard to break. Although the troubled relationship between Oppenheimer and Truman was not terminal – after all, this was the year in which Truman awarded

Oppenheimer the Presidential Medal for Merit – the wedge driven between the two men was stuck hard and fast.

MAKING ENEMIES

Despite the tensions between Oppenheimer and the President, Oppenheimer was nevertheless a figure who commanded enormous respect in the immediate aftermath of the Second World War. His diary was replete with government work. He provided technical and strategic input through the GAC from 1946 to 1952, spending much of his time at Los Alamos, Oak Ridge and other nuclear laboratories. In the process, he maintained a close connection with advances in experimental and theoretical nuclear physics. From 1947 to 1952, he also acted in various advisory capacities to the Research and Development Board of the Armed Services, a military–civilian body established under the National Security Act of

First US Atomic Energy Commission, c. 1947. Left to right: William Waymack, Lewis Strauss, David Lilienthal, Robert Backer and Sumner Pike at Oak Ridge.

The General Advisory Committee (GAC) of the Atomic Energy Commission (AEC) arrives at Santa Fe Airport, New Mexico, on 3 April 1947. Left to right: James B. Conant, J. Robert Oppenheimer, Brigadier General James McCormack, Hartley Rowe, John H. Manley, Isidor Isaac Rabi and Roger S. Warner.

1947, and provided the Secretary of Defense with scientific research advice relating to matters of national security. These duties still were not the end of his government commitments. He was on the Secretary of State's Panel on Disarmament between 1952 and 1953, and also the Science Advisory Committee between 1951 and 1954, the latter part of the Office of Defense Mobilization.

This overview of Oppenheimer's responsibilities does not do justice to the way in which his expertise was stitched through the very fabric of post-war US atomic policy-making. Given the extent and the placement of Oppenheimer's government work, he was clearly in an ideal position to wield influence over post-war nuclear thought. 'When you open any door in Washington, Oppenheimer's in that room,' said Dr Michael Gordin, a historian of science at Princeton.[91]

As if Oppenheimer was not busy enough, from 1945 his academic career also took off once more, freed from the constraints of his wartime responsibilities. He received and accepted several invitations to participate in think-tanks and policy bodies, such as the Council of the National Academy of Science, the Board of Overseers of Harvard, and the Committee on the Present Danger. (As a significant counterbalance to the idea that Oppenheimer was a closet communist, the latter organization was an anti-communist think-tank.) Immediately after the end of wartime hostilities,

Frank Oppenheimer became a respected physicist in his own right, but his historical involvement with left-wing ideology caused problems for both him and his brother in the 1940s and 50s.

Oppenheimer also resumed teaching at Caltech, but within a year lost interest in his work there and returned to Berkeley.

In December 1947, Oppenheimer was offered a role that would accompany him for the rest of his life. The position was that of director of the Institute for Advanced Study (IAS), a pioneering academic research institute founded in Princeton in 1930. (The IAS was, and remains, independent from Princeton University, but enjoys close collaborative ties.) The person making the offer to Oppenheimer will become crucial to our ongoing story. He was Lewis Strauss. Strauss was an influential figure on campus and in politics. Not only was he a trustee of the IAS, but he also happened to be a sitting member on the AEC. He was exactly the type of person with whom Oppenheimer should have built a solid alliance. Instead, Strauss became Oppenheimer's most vitriolic and committed opponent.

But that was some years away. In late 1947, Oppenheimer took some time to reflect upon Strauss's offer. At that time, the IAS was not the most prestigious destination for someone of Oppenheimer's calibre. It did, however, offer him the opportunity to build something from scratch, a new and pioneering centre for American physics. So after mulling it over, he accepted Strauss's offer. Oppenheimer would be the third director of the IAS, serving it faithfully until 1966. Under his guidance, the IAS gained an enviable reputation for research excellence. He promoted a stimulating interdisciplinary approach to studies, cross-fertilizing ideas and innovations.

As he had demonstrated at Los Alamos, Oppenheimer could be a tireless recruiter. He brought some of the world's foremost physicists to the IAS, while also promoting a new generation of brilliant students. His directorship demonstrated those qualities that had made his leadership at Los Alamos such a success; he knew how to acquire and foster talent and bring people together in collaborative excitement, his own intellect at the hub of the network.

Oppenheimer was not the only one satisfied by his move to the IAS. Kitty also welcomed the relocation to Princeton, not least because of the handsome accommodation that came with Oppenheimer's position. Their relationship had survived Oppenheimer's affair with Tatlock, but he apparently remained romantically restless. During the later war years, or shortly thereafter, Oppenheimer appears to have struck up another relationship with Ruth Tolman, simultaneously jeopardizing both his marriage and one of his closest friendships, that with Ruth's husband Richard. Ruth was compelling for Oppenheimer. She was a brilliant and attractive woman, with an impressive career in psychiatry. Oppenheimer was drawn to both her intellect and her intuitive warmth. The exact nature of their secretive connection is unclear. It appears likely that they had an emotional affair only, not a sexual one, although there is a deep intensity and longing in their letters to one another. Their affectionate bond would continue for several years, even after Richard's tragic sudden death of a heart attack in August 1948.

THE WORLD TURNS

On 29 August 1949, the Soviet Union exploded its first atomic weapon. The shock among the US political and defence establishment, and among wider American society, was pronounced. The USA was now no longer in an exclusive one-member club of atomic powers. (The United Kingdom also joined the club in October 1952.) Having so recently fought a world war, humanity once again teetered on the abyss of global conflict. The tensions between communism and capitalism were inscribing deep ideological lines across the map of the world. Much of Eastern Europe was now under communist rule, either directly within an expanded Soviet Union (e.g. Latvia, Lithuania and Estonia) or part of the Soviet-aligned communist Eastern Bloc, which included Albania, Bulgaria, Czechoslovakia, East Germany, Hungary, Poland, Romania and Yugoslavia. (The entire European communist landmass was later formalized in 1955 as the Warsaw Pact.) Democracy across this vast extent of territory was eradicated. But the Soviet Union was not the only powerful communist actor on the planet. In East Asia, the Chinese Communist Party (CCP) prevailed in the interminable Chinese Civil War; in 1949, Mao Zedong established the People's Republic of China (PRC). The following year, communist North Korea invaded US-backed South Korea, triggering three years of conventional warfare between a UN army (led and dominated by the USA) and North Korean and, eventually, Chinese communist forces. A similar struggle was playing out in French Indochina between French colonial forces and Viet Minh communist insurgents under the legendary Ho Chi Minh, a conflict that progressively slipped from the French grasp and terminated in a communist victory in 1954. The Korean War had ended the year before in an unsatisfying stalemate.

On 7 April 1954, the US President Dwight D. Eisenhower gave a news conference in which he consolidated international developments into a single guiding fear, the 'domino theory': 'Finally, you have broader considerations that might follow what you would call the "falling domino" principle. You have a row of dominoes set up, you knock over the first one, and what will happen to the last one is the certainty that it will go over very quickly. So you could have a beginning of a disintegration that would have the most profound influences.'[92]

Eisenhower, and many of his mindset, saw communism like a polluting patch of oil, spreading insidiously from one country to its neighbour, in the process smothering civil liberties, democracy and personal wealth. In this context, the atomic bomb had, in just four short years, gone from being a war-winning weapon to a guarantor of ongoing US military supremacy. But now the Soviets had the bomb. It was therefore part of a much wider diplomatic and strategic game, one in which national security was precariously guaranteed by what was later called 'mutually assured destruction'.

The Cold War was as much a cultural struggle as it was a political and military competition. In the USA, the 1940s and 1950s in particular were the time of the 'Red Scare', a pathological fear that communism would undermine and supplant the American way of life. An anxious press continually gnawed on the possibilities of homegrown spies and sleeper agents. The general paranoia led to the establishment of the House Un-American Activities Committee (HUAC) in 1946 and also to US Senator Joseph McCarthy's histrionic and aggressive campaign to root out communist sympathizers from American culture between 1950 and 1954. It should be said, however, that concern about Soviet espionage was not entirely misplaced. The early 1950s unmasked a network of Soviet spies deep in the Western establishment, including within the wartime Manhattan Project. Ideologically driven individuals such as Klaus Fuchs, Theodore Hall, David Greenglass, and Julius and Ethel Rosenberg willingly and persistently passed information to the communists, aiding and accelerating the Soviet atomic programme. For the security services there was an important lesson – keep your eye on the scientists.

And this included Oppenheimer. The post-war FBI surveillance on Oppenheimer would become unrelenting, accessing his home, his telephones, his offices, his documents, his acquaintances. Ironically, Oppenheimer was perfectly aware of the 'covert' surveillance. Later FBI transcripts of phone conversations between Oppenheimer and Kitty included the couple joking about the fact that the FBI were almost certainly listening across the wires. Despite their efforts, the FBI would never find the smoking gun. They would collect enough, however, to oil the wheels of his downfall as a nuclear scientist.

THE BATTLE OF THE 'SUPER'

One point needs to be made clear – Oppenheimer was not anti nuclear weapons, even after he saw what they could do against Japan. He had deep concerns about how they were controlled, produced, stockpiled, monitored and managed. He feared the potential destruction they could wreak on humanity. But at no point did he switch to a pacifist position. Early in the 1950s, he even suggested to Edward Teller that nuclear weapons could be used as a means to end the Korean War.

But nor does this mean that he was perfectly aligned with the interests of the US military-industrial complex. In fact, it was his adverse relationship to a specific form of nuclear weapon – the hydrogen bomb or 'Super' – that would have devastating consequences for his government career. Two figures above others will dominate the subsequent part of Oppenheimer's story – Edward Teller and Lewis Strauss.

During the war, while legions of others within the Manhattan Project were focused on the fission bomb, Teller had switched his focus (with Oppenheimer's approval) to the H-bomb. It became his principal passion and drive, and after the war he remained at Los Alamos to pursue his work further. Other great physicists and mathematicians were drawn into the orbit of his project, including Stanisław Ulam, John von Neumann, Enrico Fermi, Richard Garwin, Herbert York and Norris Bradbury. He also had the support of Lewis Strauss.

Strauss knew how to get things done in Washington. Having started his working life as a shoe salesman, he eventually achieved financial empowerment as an investment banker and then political success working for the US Food Administration and the American Relief Administration. During the Second World War, he was employed in the US Navy's Department of Ordnance as a leader in weapons development. Given the breadth of his experience, his appointment to the AEC in 1946 was a judicious move. He worked the position well, with Eisenhower naming him as a presidential advisor on atomic energy in 1953, the same year in which he became chairman of the AEC.

Strauss was accustomed to power, but he could also be bureaucratic, sensitive to his public image and, crucially, capable of building deep and pathological resentment towards those who thwarted him or dared to belittle him. One former AEC commissioner said of Strauss: 'If you disagree with Lewis about anything, he assumes you're just a fool at first. But if you go on disagreeing with him, he concludes you must be a traitor.'[93] Hold that in mind.

Teller and his colleagues became locked in an increasingly acrimonious debate among the community of nuclear scientists, politicians and military leaders. On one side were Teller and his supporters vigorously arguing for the pursuit and development of the H-bomb as an instrument of national policy, regardless of the considerable technical challenges and moral questions. On the other side were those who, with equal determination, were opposed to the Super. They included Oppenheimer. The two pivotal questions that hung over this debate were: Can you build one? Should you build one?

It was during this period that Oppenheimer began to make enemies. In June 1949 Oppenheimer appeared before HUAC and testified against a fellow scientist, Bernard Peters, accusing him of being a communist. The accusation cost Peters his job at the University of Rochester, but also cost Oppenheimer the respect of many in the scientific community. Furthermore, Frank Oppenheimer, who at this time was an assistant professor of physics at the University of Minnesota, was himself interrogated publicly by

the HUAC panel. Every communist association was dragged into the open, but Frank's misery was compounded by the fact that his brother did not publicly support him afterwards. Oppenheimer was becoming isolated.

We return to Strauss. His falling-out with Oppenheimer began in 1947, when they clashed over the issue of the export of isotopes, which were by-products of nuclear reactor processes. At this

Edward Teller poses for a security photo, Los Alamos, 1940s.

time, the USA had authorized the export of isotopes to approved foreign countries for medical and scientific research. Strauss was very much opposed to this market, believing that the isotopes could be used for military purposes. Oppenheimer disagreed and Strauss was out-voted on the issue in the AEC. The seeds of enmity were thus planted. They grew in 1949 when the debate about isotopes came to a head in a public, very public, congressional hearing. Strauss put forward his position, which was then crushed by Oppenheimer with considerable polish, humour and the full superiority of his scientific knowledge. Effectively, Strauss had been mocked. Those watching Strauss appeared almost terrified by what they saw. One of them, Lilienthal, said: 'There was a look of hatred there that you don't often see in a man's face.'[94]

Strauss's bruised fury was augmented by the continuing battle over the development of the Super. Following detonation of the Soviet atomic bomb in 1949, Teller was even more compelled to drive the H-bomb forward, but that would require presidential approval. Oppenheimer was one of the most significant blockers in this regard (among others – the internal politics of this period are complex). Explosive meetings within the GAC and AEC culminated in a GAC report on 30 October 1949. In it, the GAC appeared hawkish on some matters, including scaling up production of fissile materials and related manufacturing facilities. The report also stated: 'The General Advisory Committee recommends to the Commission an intensification of efforts to make atomic weapons available for tactical purposes, and to give attention to the problem of integration of bomb and carrier design in this field.'[95]

The crucial word here is tactical. By placing the emphasis on the battlefield use of atomic weapons, rather than the city-destroying strategic use, the GAC report was in effect positioning itself against the Super, a point that becomes explicit later on in the document:

> The General Advisory Committee has considered at great length the question of whether to pursue with high priority the development of the super bomb. No member of the Committee was willing to endorse this proposal. The reasons for our views leading to this conclusion stem in large part from the technical nature of the super and of the work necessary to establish it as a weapon. [...] We are all reluctant to see the United States take the initiative in precipitating this development. We are all agreed that it would be wrong at the present moment to commit ourselves to an all-out effort toward its development.[96]

Elsewhere in the report, however, came the admission that there was division and dissension over the issue of the Super, but it was clear what side Oppenheimer was on. Oppenheimer repeatedly argued that the Super was a technical challenge that could not be met, or could be met only with the distracting and wasteful diversion of massive resources. Plus the city-shattering power of the Super raised deep moral questions about the safety of humanity. What was the Super for?

Publication of the report would not put the issue in abeyance. In fact, Teller, Strauss, Fermi and influential others marshalled the full scope of their back-channel resources and eventually won the day. On 31 January 1950, President Truman (who was President until January 1953, when Eisenhower took office) announced the official government programme for the development of the H-bomb. It proved as successful as the Manhattan Project. On

1 November 1952, the 'Ivy Mike' thermonuclear bomb exploded over Elugelab island, Enewetak Atoll in the Pacific. It had a yield of 10.4 *megatons*, which made it nearly 700 times more powerful than the bomb dropped on Hiroshima.

Oppenheimer was now on the wrong side of history. He also began to seem to be on the wrong side of the science. Many individuals and key groups began to view him with either suspicion at best or hostility at worst. They included commanding bodies such as the US Air Force, who turned on Oppenheimer after he made policy arguments that would have affected their control of strategic atomic weaponry. But more problematic for Oppenheimer was that Strauss and others began to see darker motives in Oppenheimer's obstruction of the H-bomb.

Strauss was well aware of Oppenheimer's historical socialist leanings and communist associations, and of his extramarital affairs, and loathed him the more for them. Strauss also noted that in an article written for the July 1953 edition of *Foreign Affairs*, Oppenheimer stated that the Soviet development of a thermonuclear bomb was running about four years behind the progress of the USA. That statement was shattered when the Soviet Union tested its own H-bomb on 12 August 1953 in Kazakhstan. Was Oppenheimer, Strauss considered, attempting to deflect American attention from the Soviet weapons programme? Strauss was additionally concerned to discover that Oppenheimer had opposed the long-range airborne detection system that was used to discover that the Soviets had conducted their first atomic test back in 1949. At the very least, Strauss was questioning the value of Oppenheimer's judgement. At worst, he started to see Oppenheimer as a potential security threat. The latter appetite was fed by Teller, who testified to the FBI that Oppenheimer had willingly attempted to delay the development of the H-bomb, potentially on 'direct orders from Moscow'.

With Strauss's facilitation and backing, surveillance on Oppenheimer and scrutiny of his past intensified, at the same time as Oppenheimer was also attracting plenty of adverse press for his positions on strategic issues. The culmination of the intelligence efforts was a letter composed by William L. Borden, the Secretary of the Joint Congressional Committee on Atomic Energy, sent to J. Edgar Hoover on 7 November 1953. The letter's key conclusion couldn't have been starker: 'The purpose of this letter is to state my own exhaustively considered opinion, based upon years of study, of the available classified evidence, that more probably than not J. Robert Oppenheimer is an agent of the Soviet Union.'[97]

It was a devastating accusation, electrified by the pathological anti-communism of the times and the nuclear arms race that was emerging between East and West. The FBI began to collect and distribute the information on Oppenheimer's file, including to the President's office.

Strauss had a strong hand to play. He noted that Oppenheimer's contract as a consultant to the AEC, via the GAC, was due to expire at the end of June 1953. The renewal of that contract would also require the renewal of Oppenheimer's top-level security clearance, to which Strauss and others were now vehemently opposed. They had found a way to bring Oppenheimer down.

On 18 December 1953, Strauss, in his capacity as chairman of the AEC, met with Vice President Richard Nixon and the head of the CIA, Allen Dulles. Oppenheimer was the topic of conversation. It was agreed that he was a potential security threat, and a large battery of charges were marshalled against him. They decided to remove Oppenheimer's security clearance immediately and present him with two choices in response to the specified charges: resign from his position on the AEC or appeal against his suspension in front of a security panel.

On 21 December 1953, Oppenheimer was called into a meeting at Strauss's office on Constitution Avenue in Washington DC. There he was met by Strauss, in the company of General Kenneth Nichols, the AEC general manager. An apparently nervous Strauss informed Oppenheimer of his security suspension and presented him with a detailed list of accusations, 24 in total. Oppenheimer would have recognized that there was little new here. Most of the charges related to long-winded rehashing of his past left-wing associations, but a single point also highlighted his opposition to development of the hydrogen bomb. The following give a taste of the charges, which ran to many pages:

The substance of the information which raises the question concerning your eligibility for employment on Atomic Energy Commission work is as follows:

It was reported that in 1940 you were listed as a sponsor of the Friends of the Chinese People, an organization which was characterized in 1944 by the House Committee on Un-American Activities as a Communist front-organization. It was further reported that in 1940 your name was included on a letterhead of the American Committee for Democratic and Intellectual Freedom as a member of its national executive committee. The American Committee for Democracy and Intellectual Freedom characterized in 1942 by the House Committee on Un-American Activities as a Communist front which defended Communist teachers, and in 1943 it was characterized as subversive and un-American by a special subcommittee of the House Committee on Appropriations. [...]

It was reported that in 1943 and previously you were intimately associated with Dr. Jean Tatlock, a member of the Communist Party in San Francisco, and that Dr. Tatlock was partially responsible for your association with Communist front-groups.

It was reported that your wife, Katherine Puening Oppenheimer, was formerly the wife of Joseph Dallet, a member of the Communist Party, who was killed in Spain in 1937 fighting for the Spanish Republican Army. It was further reported that during the period of her association with Joseph Dallet, your wife became a member of the Communist Party. The Communist Party has been designated by the Attorney General as a subversive organization which seeks to alter the form of government of the United States by unconstitutional means, within the purview of Executive Order 9835 and Executive Order 10450.

[...]

It was reported that in 1945 you expressed the view that 'there is a reasonable possibility that it (the hydrogen bomb) can be made', but that the feasibility of the hydrogen bomb did not appear, on theoretical grounds, as certain as the fission bomb appeared certain, on theoretical grounds, when the Los Alamos Laboratory was started; and that in the autumn of 1949 the General Advisory

Committee expressed the view that 'an imaginative and concerted attack on the problem has a better than even chance of producing the weapon within 5 years.' It was further reported that in the autumn of 1949, and subsequently, you strongly opposed the development of the hydrogen bomb; (1) on moral grounds, (2) by claiming that it was not feasible, (3) by claiming that there were insufficient facilities and scientific personnel to carry on the development, and (4) that it was not politically desirable.[98]

The cautious opening phrasing of each point – 'It was reported' – remind us that Oppenheimer was not being presented with *criminal* charges, nor was he being arrested. His life, liberty and pursuit of happiness were not at risk. Rather, the accusations were an aggregation of suspicion, the totality of which meant that in the eyes of the investigators Oppenheimer's character was no longer fit for purpose at the heart of the nuclear programme:

In view of your access to highly sensitive classified information, and in view of these allegations which, until disproved, raise questions as to your veracity, conduct and even your loyalty, the Commission has no other recourse, in discharge of its obligations to protect the common defense and security, but to suspend your clearance until the matter has been resolved. Accordingly, your employment on Atomic Energy Commission work and your eligibility for access to restricted data are hereby suspended, effective immediately, pending final determination of this matter.[99]

Oppenheimer had not seen this coming. Stunned and dejected, he retreated from the meeting to consider his options. He was given a little time to think over his response. Some of those around him advised him to take the option of resignation, arguing quite plausibly that the result of the security hearing was effectively an adverse foregone conclusion, rubber-stamping Strauss's intentions. Going through the hearing would simply be self-inflicted torture. But Oppenheimer was not a person to relinquish his status or reputation easily. His response letter read:

> I have thought most earnestly of the alternative suggested [his resignation]. Under the circumstances this course of action would mean that I accept and concur in the view that I am not fit to serve this government, that I have now served for some twelve years. This I cannot do. If I were thus unworthy I could hardly have served our country as I have tried or been the director of our Institute in Princeton or have spoken, as on more than one occasion I have found myself speaking, in the name of our science and our country.[100]

Oppenheimer's case would therefore go to a full security hearing.

THE CASE AGAINST J. ROBERT OPPENHEIMER

Seen in the full light of present-day information, J. Robert Oppenheimer's hearing before the Personnel Security Board in Washington DC between 12 April and 6 May 1954 could hardly be called an exercise in due process. As we have already ascertained, by this stage Oppenheimer had amassed opponents significant in both status and volume. The cards were stacked against him from the outset.

The panel of men who would examine his case were all AEC appointees, chaired by the former Secretary of the Army Gordon Gray, who now held the position of president of the University of North Carolina. The cross-examination of Oppenheimer and witnesses would be led by Special Counsel Roger Robb. Robb was a very deliberate choice, a man whose professional character would define the spirit of the proceedings. He was an aggressively combative Washington prosecutor. One biographer of Oppenheimer, Robert Jungk, said of Robb that 'He did not treat Oppenheimer as a witness in his own case but as a person charged with high treason.'[101]

Oppenheimer, by contrast, was represented principally by the genteel Wall Street attorney Lloyd K. Garrison, a man with a far more restrained demeanour compared to Robb. Garrison's appointment ran against the recommendation of Joe Volpe, a former AEC lawyer, who sensing what was ahead recommended that Oppenheimer get himself a hardened litigator. Garrison would be hobbled further by his own lack of security clearance by the AEC. This meant that he was not allowed to see the confidential documents on which many of the charges were based, either in session or in advance. He therefore could not prepare defensive arguments in response to these documents; he simply had to respond to Robb's quotation from them in the hearing room – Robb was, naturally, given the respective clearance. Furthermore, throughout the trial Oppenheimer would remain under FBI surveillance and monitoring, which meant that his discussions with Garrison and his views of the proceedings could be related to the opposition.

The security hearings were a grinding, prolonged affair. To give a sense of their extent, a highly redacted version of the transcript was released in June 1954 – it ran to 1,011 pages. When the full declassified transcript was released more than 60 years later, it consisted of 25 individual volumes plus one substantial 'Record of Deletions'. The case brought 38 witnesses in front of the panel, including Nobel prize winners such as Rabi and Fermi, representing various angles of opinion on Oppenheimer. Kitty was dutifully supportive of her husband throughout, and indeed was asked to give testimony. She did this competently, but the hearing was also a painful experience for her, as revelations about Tatlock were paraded and analyzed. The media was not allowed into the hearings – they took place behind closed doors in a basic office room near the Washington Monument housing offices of the AEC. But given Oppenheimer's public status, media interest was running hot, and full attention was brought to bear on the man with the pork-pie hat.

The daily twists and turns of Oppenheimer's security hearings are too great to analyze in depth here, but some highlights illustrate the nature of the ordeal for Oppenheimer. One of the most devastating witnesses to speak against Oppenheimer was Edward Teller, who came to the hearings with an axe to grind. In the following Q&A section, Teller managed to be both evasive and incisive:

Q To simplify the issues here, perhaps, let me ask you this question: Is it your intention in anything that you are about to testify to, to suggest that Dr. Oppenheimer is disloyal to the United States?
A I do not want to suggest anything of the kind. I know Oppenheimer as an intellectually most alert and a very complicated person, and I think it would be presumptuous

and wrong on my part if I would try in any way to analyze his motives. But I have always assumed, and I now assume that he is loyal to the United States. I believe this, and I shall believe it until I see very conclusive proof to the opposite.

Q Now, a question which is the corollary of that. Do you or do you not believe that Dr. Oppenheimer is a security risk?

A In a great number of cases I have seen Dr. Oppenheimer act – I understood that Dr. Oppenheimer acted – in a way which for me was exceedingly hard to understand. I thoroughly disagreed with him in numerous issues and his actions frankly appeared to me confused and complicated. To this extent I feel that I would like to see the vital interests of this country in hands which I understand better, and therefore trust more. In this very limited sense I would like to express a feeling that I would feel personally more secure if public matters would rest in other hands.[102]

The last sentence here, perhaps better than any other in the transcript, sums up the heart of the move against Oppenheimer by the AEC. Teller seems to argue *against* the possibility of Oppenheimer as an outright spy. But within the same breath, he views him as a potential security risk because Oppenheimer's actions, perspectives and character do not align with the best interests of the USA.

The evidence presented about communist connections was crucial to the case built by Robb, Strauss and others. But while that evidence could be uncomfortable for Oppenheimer, in itself it was not decisive. Through the testimony of people such as Teller, therefore, Robb was able to build a more general unease about Oppenheimer's suitability for work with the AEC.

Oppenheimer's experience of giving testimony to the hearing, which included ad hominem attacks on his character, was deeply unpleasant. Reading over the transcripts, there are many times where Oppenheimer's legendary eloquence and logic seemed to stumble under the wearying assault on his personal history and his private behaviour. Here, for example, is just a short excerpt from the prolonged questioning he received over the Eltenton/Chevalier affair:

Q In your answer to page 22, referring to the Eltenton episode: 'It has long been clear to me that I should have reported the incident at once.'

A It is.

Q 'The events that led me to report it, which I doubt ever would have become known without my report, were unconnected with it.' You have told us that your discussion with Colonel Lansdale encompassed the subject of espionage. Of course, you have told us also that the Eltenton matter involved espionage; is that correct?

A Let's be careful. The word espionage was not mentioned.

Q No?

A The word indiscretion was mentioned. That is all that Lansdale said. Indiscretion was talking to unauthorized people who in turn would talk to other people. This is all I was told. [...]

Q So, Doctor, it is not quite correct to say that the Eltenton incident was not connected with your talk with Lansdale, is it?

A I didn't mean it in that sense. I meant that it had nothing to do with Chevalier or Eltenton with respect to the events that aroused this.

Q But your talk with Lansdale did have to do with the subject which included Chevalier and Eltenton, didn't it?

A I have described it as well as I can. Chevalier's name was not mentioned; Eltenton's name was not mentioned; and espionage was not mentioned.

Q I didn't say that. But it had to do with the subject which involved Chevalier or at least Eltenton?

A Sure, that is why I brought it up?

Q What did you tell Lieutenant Johnson about this when you first mentioned Eltenton to him?

A I had two interviews and therefore I am not clear as to which was which.

Q May I help you?

A Please.

Q I think your first interview with Johnson was quite brief, was it not?

A That is right. I think I said little more than that Eltenton was somebody to worry about.

Q Yes.

A Then I was asked why I did say this. Then I invented a cock and bull story.[103]

Oppenheimer's admission that he had constructed a 'cock and bull story' played musically to those who wanted to destabilize Oppenheimer's authority. On this basis, they could argue that Oppenheimer was definitely not the right stuff to advise the US government on critical nuclear security issues.

As many of Oppenheimer's confidants had predicted before the hearings even began, Strauss eventually got his way. On 27 May, the board presented its final conclusions. Notably, they top-ended their verdict by asserting that Oppenheimer should be regarded as a 'loyal citizen' to the USA. Certainly, none of the testimony or documentation illustrated that Oppenheimer was traitorous to any degree; he had just had an intellectually stimulating and varied life, one that placed him in contact with ideas and people problematic in a new ideological age. But loyalty to country was not enough:

> We have, however, been unable to arrive at the conclusion that it would be clearly consistent with the security interests of the United States to reinstate Dr. Oppenheimer's clearance and, there-fore, do not so recommend.
>
> The following considerations have been controlling in lead-ing us to our conclusion:
>
> We find that Dr. Oppenheimer's continuing conduct and associa-tions have reflected a serious disregard for the requirements of the security system.
>
> We have found a susceptibility to influence which could have seri-ous implications for the security interests of the country.
>
> We find his conduct in the hydrogen-bomb program sufficiently disturbing as to raise a doubt as to whether his future participa-tion, if characterized by the same attitudes in a Government pro-gram relating to the national defense, would be clearly consistent with the best interests of security.
>
> We have regretfully concluded that Dr. Oppenheimer has been

less than candid in several instances in his testimony before this Board.[104]

So it was, after what amounted to a month-long character assassination, that Oppenheimer's work on nuclear weaponry and national security came to an end. But the future remained. The 'Father of the Atom Bomb' now needed to look beyond the greatness of his wartime work, recover, and find new horizons.

CHAPTER 6

REINCARNATION

As the spring of 1954 rolled into the summer, the immediate drama of Oppenheimer's security clearance hearing was behind him. The question that remained was, What now? Oppenheimer still had gainful employment with the IAS. But we are reminded that it was none other than Lewis Strauss – the man who more than any other brought Oppenheimer's nuclear science career to an end – who sat on the IAS board of trustees. Would Strauss now make a move against Oppenheimer's academic career?

Albert Einstein and Oppenheimer had a fluctuating personal and professional relationship, but were closer during the last decade of Einstein's life, between 1945 and 1955.

TURNING POINT

Oppenheimer was vulnerable at this time, psychologically bruised by the ordeal he had just endured. Physicist Hans Bethe, one of those who testified in defence of Oppenheimer during the hearings, reflected that 'Oppenheimer took the outcome of the security hearing very quietly but he was a changed person; much of his previous spirit and liveliness had left him.'[105] Students and staff at the IAS noticed how much older he looked than just a few months previously. The attention placed upon him was also withering to his spirit. FBI surveillance was still active, the Bureau refusing to let him go. There were also long column inches devoted to Oppenheimer in the press, analyzing his life, character, relationships and achievements. Oppenheimer clearly needed some space.

But it was from the public domain that the turnaround came. The year 1954 was pivotal in terms of the broad American attitude towards the virulent anti-communism that had been pulsing within the USA since 1950. The antipathy towards communist ideology remained, but among the wider society there was a growing aversion to its more extreme expressions, its gleeful persecution. The world had particularly turned against Joseph McCarthy, for example, not least because he ill-advisedly widened his list of enemies to include respected figures such as the Protestant clergy and the US Army. But there was also a turn against the unforgiving spite of his campaign. McCarthy's popularity plunged, especially after his position was demolished by the respected TV journalist Edward R. Murrow on the influential documentary series *See It Now*. McCarthy's subsequent fall from grace was rapid, his reputation effectively demolished by a Congressional rebuke in December 1954.

We can speculate that Strauss would also have been aware of the turning tide. In relation to Oppenheimer's position with the IAS, it was important that he appeared magnanimous rather than vindictive. Strauss at first opted to delay a decision about the renewal of Oppenheimer's directorship of the Institute. But the rest of the board was solidly in favour of retaining Oppenheimer. He was proving excellent at his job and, at least since the end of the security hearings, he was sinking even more time into making the IAS the strongest expression of itself. Thus in October 1954, Oppenheimer's directorship was renewed, Strauss apparently siding with the decision.

Oppenheimer's future career is our main focus from this point on, but it is worth noting the impact of the aftermath of the security hearings on Strauss's career. After the hearings, many in the scientific community collected themselves to protest against what they saw as the appalling treatment of a man who had served his country dutifully. At Los Alamos, a junior physicist called Fred L. Ribe (a future professor of nuclear engineering at the University of Washington) wrote a letter of protest accompanied by a petition signed by 492 fellow scientists, who put their names on the petition at some risk to their own reputation. The documents were sent to Eisenhower and the AEC on 7 June 1954, expressing how 'deeply disturbed' they were by the handling of one of their own:

The board has found Dr. Oppenheimer to be a loyal and discreet citizen who had made unusual contributions to the security of our country. The nature of the argument by which the majority of the board nevertheless concludes that he is a security risk is alarming. For example, the new requirement of enthusiastic conformity has no place in an American personnel security system. We feel that a man can give no better proof of his devotion to the security of our country than has Dr. Oppenheimer by his record over the past twelve years.[106]

The civil liberties arguments expressed here began to hold far more sway within the American public as the 1950s progressed. Strauss found himself on the wrong side of the public mood. He had also fallen out of favour with many political figures, the outcome of policy battles over various government issues. After his chairmanship of the AEC ended in 1958, a struggle ensued as the President attempted to appoint Strauss to the position of Secretary of Commerce. The opposition that was now gathered against Strauss ultimately stopped his nomination and effectively ended Strauss's political career.

Oppenheimer, Kitty and Toni visit the Acropolis in Athens, Greece, 28 May 1958.

Oppenheimer, meanwhile, continued to demonstrate loyalty to a country that in many ways had treated him so badly. Academic possibilities abroad were plentiful, including among some of the most prestigious physics institutes in Europe. Oppenheimer pursued none of them. When he was asked by the US diplomat George Kennan why he stayed within the USA, Oppenheimer replied, apparently with tears in his eyes, 'Dammit, I love this country.'[107]

With the confirmation of his position as director of the IAS, Oppenheimer could now invest all his time back into his first love, science, free from the pressures of government responsibility. This trajectory proved to be an enormous blessing, both for Oppenheimer and for the world at large. Once the immediate trauma of the security clearance hearings had subsided, many people noticed that Oppenheimer appeared quieter, more reflective, even peaceful. His underlying enthusiasm for the subject of physics reignited in earnest and along with it came an apparently renewed passion for transferring his knowledge to students, fellow scientists and the public at large.

The next 12 years of Oppenheimer's life saw him dedicate himself to public speaking and creative instruction. His diary became crammed with speaking engagements on many different topics. But this was not just a scientist speaking to an elite specialist audience. Rather, in Oppenheimer's last decade he found an inspirational poetry in his public speaking that chimed with a public thirst for logical idealism and intellectual passion, even if they struggled to understand the concepts that he expressed. He became a public philosopher as much as a champion of physics.

Some high points of this career phase are worth emphasizing. We should of course note that Oppenheimer's gift for graceful public speaking certainly predated the security clearance hearings. In 1953, for example, Oppenheimer gave six lectures as part of the BBC Reith Lectures in the UK. (The Reith Lectures are a prestigious and internationally respected annual lecture programme, inaugurated in 1948 in acknowledgement of the BBC's first director general, Lord Reith.) The lectures were (and still are) broadcast on BBC Radio, so reached a particularly wide audience. Oppenheimer spoke across many aspects of quantum mechanics and atomic theory, but he also expanded upon the scientific instinct with extraordinary poetry. Here is just one short extract from the opening of lecture no. 6:

> For some moments during these lectures we have looked together into one of the rooms of the house called 'science'. This is a relatively quiet room that we know as quantum theory or atomic theory. The great girders which frame it, the lights and shadows and vast windows—these were the work of a generation our predecessor more than two decades ago. It is not wholly quiet. Young people visit it and study in it and pass on to other chambers; and from time to time someone rearranges a piece of the furniture to make the whole more harmonious; and many, as we have done, peer through its windows or walk through it as sight-seers. It is not so old but that one can hear the sound of the new wings being built nearby, where men walk high in the air to erect new scaffoldings, not unconscious of how far they may fall. All about there are busy workshops where the builders are active, and very near indeed are those of us who, learning more of the primordial structure of matter, hope some day for chambers as fair and lovely as that in which we have spent the years of our youth and our prime.[108]

Oppenheimer's analogy is beautifully crafted and sustained, a model of how to use imaginative language to gently but firmly sustain the attention of a listener. Such was the popularity of these lectures that they were subsequently published in a book entitled *Science and the Common Understanding*, published by Oxford University Press and Simon & Schuster. Given that these lectures were about theoretical physics, we can sense the personal influence Oppenheimer was exerting. The book enjoyed strong and enduring sales.

Once on the other side of the security clearance hearings, Oppenheimer's public reputation was steadily expanding, especially when he appeared upon Murrow's *See It Now* on 5 January 1955. The programme was ostensibly focused on the IAS, but its prominent and charismatic director took up much of the airtime. Significant excerpts from it can still be found online today. Oppenheimer is simply mesmerizing on camera, utterly absorbed in his subject and intensely magnetic because of it. He comes across as a man fascinated with ideas and words, painting conceptual pictures with facial expressions and precise hand gestures. The programme also brought personal insights. At one point, after a blackboard demonstration of physics, a scientifically bemused Murrow asked, 'Do you ever become frightened?' Oppenheimer replied:

> That's a real point. I only get frightened – and it happens very rarely – when I think I have an idea. That is, what people find isn't frightening, but the understanding of it sometimes has this quality. I remember a man who was my teacher in Göttingen, he is in Chicago now, James Franck, he said, 'The only way I can tell whether my thoughts really have some weight to them is the sense of terror when I think of something new.'[109]

Even allowing for the fact that Oppenheimer anchors his answer upon a quotation, his sincerity feels transparent. We sense the camera, and the audience, leaning into his words and his undiluted passion for ideas, daring others to raise their sights.

See It Now catapulted Oppenheimer into the limelight. Public demand for his lectures was apparently insatiable, with many hundreds, sometimes thousands, attending scientific lectures that were utterly opaque to many in the audience. For example, in April 1955 Oppenheimer lectured on 'The Sub-Nuclear Zoo: The Constitution of Matter' at Oregon State University. While we might expect an audience consisting of a few dozen senior academics, in fact 2,500 people attended, most of them members of a baffled but equally beguiled public.

Such events were repeated across the USA in the second half of the 1950s and in the first half of the 1960s. Oppenheimer also toured widely abroad. Countries he visited on speaking and teaching engagements included Belgium, Denmark, Canada, France, Germany, Switzerland and the UK. From 1961 he also lectured widely across South America under the prestigious Professorship Program of the Organization of American States (OAS), whose members brusquely ignored complaints from some members of the US Congress, those who were still doggedly aligned against Oppenheimer's public success.

The international trip followed most closely, however, was surely that he made to Japan in September 1960, accompanied by his wife Kitty. He was there as a guest of the Japan Committee of Intellectual Interchange. As we would expect, press conferences in Japan led to questions about whether Oppenheimer regretted the part he played in the development and deployment of the atomic bomb during the Second World War. Oppenheimer replied rather awkwardly: 'I do not regret that I had something to do with the technical success of the atomic bomb. It isn't that I don't feel bad; it is that I don't feel worse tonight than I did last night.'[110] The

In front of a bust of Niels Bohr, Oppenheimer speaks at the inauguration of the Nuclear Physics Institute at the Weizmann Institute of Science in Israel, 1958.

moral complexity of some topics could still challenge Oppenheimer's otherwise sublime powers of speech.

But the public on the whole wrapped their arms around Oppenheimer. They listened carefully as he spoke about the wonder for science and the need for humanity to speak freely, share ideas, test solutions, play with theories. He had an insider's insight into what happens when minds are shuttered. In an age in which freedom of speech was under assault globally, he had a powerful appeal.

END STATE

It would take some time before governmental injustices were righted. But that day would eventually come. Back in November 1954, President Eisenhower and the AEC had presented the great Enrico Fermi with a lifetime achievement award for his services to physics and to atomic energy. Although Fermi died shortly after, his life was remembered in 1956 when his award became the foundation of the Enrico Fermi Presidential Award. The honour would be given to those who demonstrated excellence in scientific and technological research for the benefit of wider humanity.

On the morning of 22 November 1963, a relatively new and youthful President, John F. Kennedy, approved of J. Robert Oppen-

The Fermi Award being presented to J. Robert Oppenheimer, 1963. Pictured left to right: Glenn Seaborg, Lyndon B. Johnson, Martha Parsons, J. Robert Oppenheimer, Peter Oppenheimer, Katherine 'Kitty' Oppenheimer, Claudia 'Lady Bird' Johnson, Robert Wilson, Helen L. Seaborg and James T. Ramey.

heimer's receipt of this award. Hours later, on the streets of Dallas, Texas, Kennedy was assassinated, a tragedy that plunged America into mourning. It therefore fell to another President, Lyndon B. Johnson, to present the Fermi Award to Oppenheimer, which he did on 2 December 1963 at the White House.

Even without the recent death of Kennedy, it was a poignant event. Many of Oppenheimer's friends, and some of his former foes, were gathered there. Teller, for example, was present, having endorsed Oppenheimer's nomination for the award. (Apparently Oppenheimer was guarded but friendly towards Teller, Kitty actively hostile.) Oppenheimer's citation read as follows: 'For contributions to theoretical physics as a teacher and originator of ideas and for leadership of the Los Alamos Laboratory and the atomic energy program during the critical years.' Then President Johnson spoke, granting Oppenheimer a respect that he was largely denied during those dark months of 1954:

> One of President Kennedy's most important acts was to sign the Enrico Fermi Award for Dr. Oppenheimer for his contributions to theoretical physics and the advancement of science in the United States of America.
>
> It is important to our Nation that we have constantly before us the example of men who set high standards of achievement. This has been the role that you have played, Dr. Oppenheimer.
>
> During World War Two, your great scientific and administrative leadership culminated in the forging together of many diverse ideas and experiments at Los Alamos and at other places. This successful effort came to a climax with the first atomic explosion at Alamogordo on July 16, 1945.

Since the war you have continued to lead in the search for knowledge, and you have continued to build on the major breakthrough achieved by Enrico Fermi on this day in 1942. You have led in developing an outstanding school of theoretical physics in the United States of America.

For these significant contributions, I present to you on behalf of the Atomic Energy Commission and the people of the United States the Enrico Fermi Award of 1963, the Enrico Fermi Medal.[111]

Oppenheimer appeared emotionally moved as the President spoke, holding Kitty's hand throughout. When Johnson had finished speaking, Oppenheimer offered some of his own generous words to the room:

We have not, I know, always given evidence of that brotherly spirit .... This is not because we lack vital common or intersecting scientific interests. It is in part because, with countless other men and women, we are engaged in this great enterprise of our time, testing whether men can both preserve and enlarge life, liberty, and the pursuit of happiness, and live without war as the great arbiter of history. In this enterprise, no one bears a greater responsibility than the President of the United States. I think it just possible, Mr. President, that it has taken some charity and some courage for you to make this award today. That would seem to be a good augury for all our futures.

The underpinning theme here was reconciliation, a restoration that Oppenheimer seems to have found during the rest of his life. The next three years brought Oppenheimer many plaudits and much

Top: *During a visit to Los Alamos in May 1964, Oppenheimer and his wife Kitty (centre) soberly watch 'Ten Seconds that Shook the World', a documentary about the development of the atomic bomb and the bombing of Hiroshima.*
Above: *A more relaxed moment during the Los Alamos visit.*

praise. When he turned 60 on 22 April 1964, four senior scientists from the IAS wrote their warmest tributes to Oppenheimer in that month's issue of *Review of Modern Physics*, accompanied by an equally congenial letter from an ageing Max Born. The following month, Oppenheimer and Kitty took a trip into their most intense past when they visited Los Alamos, where they found many physical changes and poignant memories. Those days, when the scientists and engineers of Los Alamos strived to win a global war and transform the future of humanity, were receding into the past, dissipating into the blowing dust.

Oppenheimer was by this stage of his life still relatively young. But problems with his health were now catching up, building themselves upon a lifetime of chain smoking. Following treatment for a serious throat and sinus infection, Oppenheimer was diagnosed with throat cancer in March 1966. Surgery, chemother-

Norris Bradbury and Oppenheimer at Los Alamos National Laboratory, 18 May 1964.

apy and radiotherapy all followed (Oppenheimer was apparently highly fascinated with the technology of the latter), but all failed to stem the progress of the disease. J. Robert Oppenheimer died on 18 February 1967 at his home at Princeton, at the age of 62. The subsequent memorial service, held in the Alexander Hall on the Princeton University campus, was attended by 600 people, after which his body was cremated and the ashes subsequently scattered by Kitty in the sea near the St John beach house.

Tragedy would bedevil the Oppenheimer family. Kitty died in October 1972 of a pulmonary embolism. Katherine Oppenheimer Silber – 'Toni' – hanged herself in the family beach house in January 1977. She was tormented not only by the failure of two marriages, but also by the fact that her career as a translator for the United Nations was stopped in its tracks when her security clearance was prohibited, on account of charges brought

Oppenheimer makes an appearance at the European Council for Nuclear Research (CERN) in 1964.

against her father by the FBI. Some enmities took a long time to die.

The legacy of most gifted scientists is often measured in terms of theories and ideas, new ways of seeing, measuring and interpreting the world. J. Robert Oppenheimer contributed at that level, certainly. But his work also altered the historical direction of our planet, profoundly so. We still live under the waxing and waning of nuclear threat, as in many ways Oppenheimer suspected we would. His work at Los Alamos was born of times so exceptional as to perhaps be unimaginable by many of us today. He performed his service to his country brilliantly, but the nature of that service was so grave that it brought both inner and outer conflict – pride and fear, respect and suspicion. In many regards, Oppenheimer is an Icarus-type figure. Starting at the confluence of mighty historical rivers, and equally magnificent scientific discoveries and theories, he took off and soared high. Greatness came at huge personal cost, but ultimately he survived and became known once again for the science he loved.

In 2023, director Christopher Nolan's film *Oppenheimer* appeared in global cinemas, to enormous interest and success. The film brought Oppenheimer to life for a modern public, many of whom previously had little interest and perhaps no knowledge of Oppenheimer's character and work. While the film was worthy of his memory, I would argue that it struggles to do justice to the full spectrum of his talent and the gifted scope of his mind. Particularly, we should remember that Oppenheimer was first and foremost a scientist – everything proceded from that. As he once said, with his talent for a lilting phrase, 'Science is not everything, but science is very beautiful.'

BIBLIOGRAPHY

Atomic Energy Commission, 'The GAC report of October 30, 1949, United States Atomic Energy Commission Washington, DC 20545 Historical Document Number 349': https://www.atomicarchive.com/resources/documents/hydrogen/gac-report.html

Bernstein, Jeremy, *Oppenheimer: Portrait of an Enigma* (Chicago: Ivan R. Dee, 2004)

Bethe, Hans, 'J. Robert Oppenheimer', in *Biographical Memoirs: Volume 71* (Washington DC: National Academy Press, 1971) pp.175–220

Bird, Kai and Martin J. Sherwin, *American Prometheus: The Triumph and the Tragedy of J. Robert Oppenheimer* (London, Atlantic Books, 2023)

Blackett, Patrick M.S., 'Nobel Lecture, December 13, 1948: Cloud Chamber Researches in Nuclear Physics and Cosmic Radiation': https://www.nobelprize.org/prizes/physics/1948/blackett/lecture/

CBS News, 'From the archives: Robert Oppenheimer in 1965 on if the bomb was necessary' (19 July 2023): https://www.youtube.com/watch?v=AdtLxlttrHg

Committee on Atomic Energy, *Report on the International Control of Atomic Energy* (Washington DC: Committee on Atomic Energy, 1946)

Einstein, Albert, 'Albert Einstein's Letter to President Franklin Delano Roosevelt'. E-World. 1997. Archived from the original on 17 April 2012. Retrieved 9 October 2013 (2 August 1939): https://en.wikipedia.org/wiki/Einstein%E2%80%93Szilard_letter#/media/File:Einstein-Roosevelt-letter.png

Elsasser, Walter M., *Memoirs of a Physicist in the Atomic Age* (London: Adam Hilger Ltd./Science History Publications, 1978)

Goodchild, Peter J., *J. Robert Oppenheimer: 'Shatterer of Worlds'* (London: BBC Books, 1980)

Greenspan, Nancy Thorndike, *The End of the Certain World* (London: Wiley, 2005) p.146

Groves, Major General Leslie R., *Memorandum for the Secretary of War: The Test* (Washington DC: War Department, 18 July 1945)

Groves, General Leslie M., *Now It Can Be Told: The Story of the Manhattan Project* (New York and Evanston, Harper & Row, 1962)

Hall, Harvey and J. R. Oppenheimer, 'Relativistic Theory of the Photoelectric Effect', *Physical Review*, 38, 57 (7 May 1941)

Herken, Gregg, *Brotherhood of the Bomb: The Tangled Lives and Loyalties of Robert Oppenheimer, Ernest Lawrence, Edward Teller* (New York: Henry Holt & Co., 2002)

Hore, Peter (ed.), *Patrick Blackett: Sailor, Scientist, Socialist* (London: Routledge, 1999)

Johnson, President Lyndon B., Presentation of Enrico Fermi Award (2 December 1963)

Joint Task Force One, 'Minutes of the meeting of the President's Evaluation Commission for the atomic bomb tests and the staff of Commander Joint Task Force One' (Washington DC: 30 March 1946)

Jungk, Robert, *Brighter than a Thousand Suns: A Personal History of the Atomic Scientists* (Boston, MA: Mariner, 1970): https://ia801309.us.archive.org/0/items/BrighterThanAThousandSuns-PersonalHistoryOfAtomicScientists/brightsun.pdf

Kuhn, Thomas S., interview with J. Robert Oppenheimer, 18 November 1963

Michelmore, Peter, *The Swift Years: The Robert Oppenheimer Story* (New York: Dodd, Mead, & Co., 1969)

Monk, Ray, *Inside the Centre: The Life of J. Robert Oppenheimer* (London: Vintage, 2013)

Musselwhite, Gia, 'After "Oppenheimer," a look back at Princeton's complicated role in nuclear history', *The Daily Princetonian* (26 July 2023): https://www.dailyprincetonian.com/article/2023/07/oppenheimer-nuclear-history-princeton-retrospective

Nichols, K.D., Letter Outlining Charges Against Robert Oppenheimer (23 December 1953): https://famous-trials.com/oppenheimer/2691-charges-against-oppenheimer-dec-23-1953

Nichols, Kenneth D., *The Road to Trinity* (New York: William Morrow and Company, 1987)

Office of the Historian, 'The Acheson–Lilienthal & Baruch Plans, 1946' (Washington DC: Department of State): https://history.state.gov/milestones/1945-1952/baruch-plans (accessed 10 May 2024)

Oppenheimer, J. Robert, 'Crossing', *Hound & Horn* (June 1928)

Oppenheimer, J. Robert, 'On the Quantum Theory of the Problem of the Two Bodies', *Mathematical Proceedings of the Cambridge Philosophical Society*, 23, 4 (October 1926) pp.422–31

Oppenheimer, J. Robert to Frank Oppenheimer, 14 October 1929

Oppenheimer, J. Robert and H. Snyder, 'On Continued Gravitational Contraction', *Physical Review*, 56, 455 (1 September 1939)

Oppenheimer, J. Robert, 'Outline of Present Knowledge' (15–24 April 1943)

Oppenheimer, J. Robert, Letter from J. Robert Oppenheimer to US Secretary of War Henry Stimson (17 August 1945)

Oppenheimer, J. Robert, Speech to the Association of Los Alamos Scientists (Los Alamos, New Mexico: 2 November 1945)

Oppenheimer, J. Robert, Acceptance speech, Army-Navy 'Excellence' Award (16 November 1945)

Oppenheimer, J. Robert, Letter to President Harry S. Truman (3 May 1946)

Oppenheimer, J. Robert, Reith Lectures 1953, 'Science and the Common Understanding – Lecture 6: The Sciences and Man's Community' (transmission 20 December 1953)

Oppenheimer, J. Robert, 'I am become Death, the destroyer of worlds.' (1965); YouTube (2012): https://www.youtube.com/watch?v=lb13ynu3Iac&t=10s

Pais, Abraham, with Robert P. Crease, *J. Robert Oppenheimer: A Life* (Oxford: Oxford University Press, 2006)

Rhodes, Richard, *The Making of the Atomic Bomb* (New York: Simon & Schuster, 1986)

Royal, Denise, *The Story of J. Robert Oppenheimer* (New York: St Martin's Press, 1969)

Serber, Robert, and E.U. Condon, *The Los Alamos Primer* (Los Alamos: Manhattan Project, 1943)

Serber, Robert, *Peace and War: Reminiscences of a Life on the Frontiers of Science* (New York: Columbia University Press, 1998)

Smith, Alice Kimball and Charles Weiner, *Robert Oppenheimer: Letters and Recollections* (Stanford: Stanford University Press, 1980)

Smith, Herbert, 'Interview of Herbert Smith by Charles Weiner on 1974 August 1, Niels Bohr Library & Archives, American Institute of Physics, College Park, MD USA': https://www.aip.org/history-programs/niels-bohr-library/oral-histories/4896

Stern, Philip M., *The Oppenheimer Case: Security on Trial* (London: Rupert Hart-Davis, 1971) p.130

'The Eternal Apprentice', *Time* magazine (4 November 1948) pp.70–81

United States Atomic Energy Commission (AEC), *In the Matter of J. Robert Oppenheimer: Transcript of Hearing before Personnel Security Board* (Washington DC: US Government Printing Office, 1954): https://www.osti.gov/opennet/hearing

US Department of Energy, Office of Scientific and Technical Information, J. Robert Oppenheimer Personnel Hearings Transcripts: https://www.osti.gov/opennet/hearing

War Department Interim Committee, Minutes, 31 May 1945

War Department Interim Committee. 'Recommendations on the Immediate Use of Nuclear Weapons', Minutes, 16 June 1945

Weisskopf, Victor F., 'The Los Alamos Years', *Physics Today*, vol. 20, issue 10 (October 1967) pp.39–42

Weisskopf, Victor F., *Physics in the Twentieth Century: Selected Essays* (Cambridge & London: The MIT Press, 1972)

ENDNOTES

1. CBS News (19 July 2023). 'From the archives: Robert Oppenheimer in 1965 on if the bomb was necessary': https://www.youtube.com/watch?v=AdtLxlttrHg

2. Quoted in Alice Kimball Smith and Charles Weiner (eds), *Robert Oppenheimer: Letters and Recollections* (Stanford, CA: Stanford University Press, 1980) p.2.

3. Quoted in Smith & Weiner, p.5.

4. Interview with J. Robert Oppenheimer by Thomas S. Kuhn, 18 November 1963.

5. Ibid.

6. Quoted in Denise Royal, *The Story of J. Robert Oppenheimer* (New York: St Martin's Press, 1969) p.23.

7. 'The Eternal Apprentice', *Time* magazine (4 November 1948) pp.70–81 (p.70).

8. Ibid., p.71.

9. Quoted in Royal, p.16.

10. Ray Monk, *Inside the Centre: The Life of J. Robert Oppenheimer* (London: Vintage, 2013) p.40.

11. Quoted in Smith & Weiner, p.6.

12. Ibid., p.7.

13. Smith, Herbert, 'Interview of Herbert Smith by Charles Weiner on 1974 August 1, Niels Bohr Library & Archives, American Institute of Physics, College Park, MD USA': https://www.aip.org/history-programs/niels-bohr-library/oral-histories/4896

14. Op. cit.

15. Op. cit.

16. Quoted in Royal, p.49.

17. Smith & Weiner, p.35.

18. Ibid., p.19.

19. Ibid., p.56.

20. Ibid., p.44.

21. Quoted in Monk, p.59.

22. Smith & Weiner, p.77.

23. Smith & Weiner, p.84.

24. Smith & Weiner, p.88.

25. Quoted in Monk, p.93.

26. Nobel Prize in Physics, Patrick M.S. Blackett, 'Nobel Lecture, December 13, 1948: Cloud Chamber Researches in Nuclear Physics and Cosmic Radiation': https://www.nobelprize.org/prizes/physics/1948/blackett/lecture/

27. Quoted in Peter Hore (ed.), *Patrick Blackett: Sailor, Scientist, Socialist* (London: Routledge, 1999) p.99.

28. Monk, pp.95–97.

29. Monk, p.98.

30. Smith & Weiner, p.98.

31. Smith & Weiner, p.92.

32. J. Robert Oppenheimer, 'On the Quantum Theory of the Problem of the Two Bodies', *Mathematical Proceedings of the Cambridge Philosophical Society*, 23, 4 (October 1926) pp.422–31.

33. Smith & Weiner, p.100.

34. Peter Michelmore, *The Swift Years: The Robert Oppenheimer Story* (New York: Dodd, Mead, & Co., 1969) p.21.

35. Walter M. Elsasser, *Memoirs of a Physicist in the Atomic Age* (London: Adam Hilger Ltd./Science History Publications, 1978) p.53.

36. Nancy Thorndike Greenspan, *The End of the Certain World* (London: Wiley, 2005) p.146.

37. Smith & Weiner, p.113.

38. J. Robert Oppenheimer, 'Crossing', *Hound & Horn* (June 1928).

39. Kai Bird and Martin J. Sherwin, *American Prometheus: The Triumph and the Tragedy of J. Robert Oppenheimer* (London, Atlantic Books, 2023) p.78.

40. Quoted in Royal, p.55.

41. Quoted in Monk, p.171.

42. J. Robert Oppenheimer to Frank Oppenheimer, 14 October 1929.

43. Quoted in Royal, p.61.

44. Smith, op. cit.

45. Smith, ibid.

46. Abraham Pais, with Robert P. Crease, *J. Robert Oppenheimer: A Life* (Oxford: Oxford University Press, 2006) p.143.

47. Ibid., pp.17–18.

48. Harvey Hall and J.R. Oppenheimer, 'Relativistic Theory of the Photoelectric Effect' *Physical Review*, 38, 57 (7 May 1941).

49. Hans Bethe, 'J. Robert Oppenheimer', in *Biographical Memoirs: Volume 71* (Washington DC: National Academy Press, 1971) pp.175–220 (p.180).

50. J.R. Oppenheimer and H. Snyder, 'On Continued Gravitational Contraction', *Physical Review*, 56, 455 (1 September 1939).

51. Jeremy Bernstein, *Oppenheimer: Portrait of an Enigma* (Chicago: Ivan R. Dee, 2004) p.48.

52. United States Atomic Energy Commission (AEC), *In the Matter of J. Robert Oppenheimer: Transcript of Hearing before Personnel Security Board* (Washington DC: US Government Printing Office, 1954).

53. Ibid.

54. Ibid.

55. Quoted in Monk, p.235.

56. AEC.

57. Personal correspondence, J. Robert Oppenheimer to Kenneth D. Nichols, March 4, 1954, in AEC, *In the Matter*.

58. AEC, *In the Matter*.

59. Quoted in Monk, p.278.

60. Robert Serber, *Peace and War: Reminiscences of a Life on the Frontiers of Science* (New York: Columbia University Press, 1998) p.58.

61. Albert Einstein, Letter to President Franklin Delano Roosevelt (2 August 1939): https://en.wikipedia.org/wiki/Einstein%E2%80%93Szilard_letter#/media/File:Einstein-Roosevelt-letter.png

62. Kenneth D. Nichols, *The Road to Trinity* (New York: William Morrow and Company, 1987) p.108.

63. AEC, p.12.

64. Letter from James B. Conant and Leslie R. Groves to J. Robert Oppenheimer, 25 February 1943.

65. General Leslie M. Groves, *Now It Can Be Told: The Story of the Manhattan Project* (New York and Evanston, Harper & Row, 1962) p.61.

66. AEC, p.130.

67. AEC, *In the Matter*.

68. Letter from Brigadier General Leslie Groves to J. Robert Oppenheimer, 29 July 1943.

69. Victor F. Weisskopf, 'Weisskopf, Victor F., 'The Los Alamos Years', *Physics Today*, vol. 20, issue 10 (October 1967)

70. Jean Tatlock, note written 4 January 1943.

71. Serber, p.86.

72. Quoted in Richard Rhodes, *The Making of the Atomic Bomb* (New York: Simon & Schuster, 1986) pp.571–72.

73. Robert Serber and E.U. Condon, *The Los Alamos Primer* (Los Alamos: Manhattan Project, 1943) p.2.

74. J. Robert Oppenheimer, 'Outline of Present Knowledge', 15–24 April 1943.

75. Memorandum for Major General L.R. Groves, 'Summary of Target Committee Meetings on 10 and 11 May 1945' (12 May 1945) p.1.

76. Ibid., p.2.

77. War Department Interim Committee, Minutes, 31 May 1945.

78. War Department Interim Committee. 'Recommendations on the Immediate Use of Nuclear Weapons', Minutes, 16 June 1945.

79. Quoted in Major General Leslie R. Groves, *Memorandum for the Secretary of War: The Test* (Washington DC: War Department, 18 July 1945).

80. Ibid.

81. J. Robert Oppenheimer, : 'I am become Death, the destroyer of worlds.' (1965) YouTube (2012): https://www.youtube.com/watch?v=lb13ynu3Iac&t=10s

82. Gregg Herken, *Brotherhood of the Bomb: The Tangled Lives and Loyalties of Robert Oppenheimer, Ernest Lawrence, Edward Teller* (New York: Henry Holt & Co., 2002) p.139.

83. Letter from J. Robert Oppenheimer to US Secretary of War Henry Stimson, 17 August 1945.

84. Quoted in Royal, p.143.

85. Quoted in Bird & Sherwin, p.332.

86. J. Robert Oppenheimer, Speech to the Association of Los Alamos Scientists (Los Alamos, New Mexico: 2 November 1945).

87. J. Robert Oppenheimer, Acceptance speech, Army-Navy 'Excellence' Award (16 November 1945).

88. Committee on Atomic Energy, *Report on the International Control of Atomic Energy* (Washington DC: Committee on Atomic Energy, 1946) pp.34–35.

89. Office of the Historian, 'The Acheson-Lilienthal & Baruch Plans, 1946' (Washington DC: Department of State): https://history.state.gov/milestones/1945-1952/baruch-plans (accessed 10 May 2024).

90. J. Robert Oppenheimer, Letter to President Harry S. Truman (3 May 1946).

91. Gia Musselwhite, 'After "Oppenheimer," a look back at Princeton's complicated role in nuclear history', *The Daily Princetonian* (26 July 2023): https://www.dailyprincetonian.com/article/2023/07/oppenheimer-nuclear-history-princeton-retrospective

92. Office of the Historian, 'Foreign Relations of the United States, 1952–1954, Indochina, Volume XIII, Part 1' (Washington DC: Department of State): https://history.state.gov/historicaldocuments/frus1952-54v13p1/d716 (accessed 12 May 2024)

93. Quoted in Bird & Sherwin, p.362, from various sources.

94. Philip M. Stern, *The Oppenheimer Case: Security on Trial* (London: Rupert Hart-Davis, 1971) p.130.

95. Atomic Energy Commission, 'The GAC report of October 30, 1949, United States Atomic Energy Commission Washington, DC 20545 Historical Document Number 349': https://www.atomicarchive.com/resources/documents/hydrogen/gac-report.html

96. Ibid.

97. Pais, p.199.

98. K.D. Nichols, Letter Outlining Charges Against Robert Oppenheimer (December 23, 1953): https://famous-trials.com/oppenheimer/2691-charges-against-oppenheimer-dec-23-1953

99. Ibid.

100. AEC, *In the Matter*.

101. Robert Jungk, *Brighter than a Thousand Suns: A Personal History of the Atomic Scientists* (Boston, MA: Mariner, 1970): https://ia801309.us.archive.org/0/items/BrighterThanAThousandSuns-PersonalHistoryOfAtomicScientists/brightsun.pdf

102. AEC, *In the Matter*: https://famous-trials.com/oppenheimer/2706-testimony-of-dr-edward-teller-in-the-oppenheimer-hearing

103. AEC, *In the Matter*: https://famous-trials.com/oppenheimer/2702-oppenheimer-testimony-on-the-chevalier-eltenton-incident

104. AEC, *In the Matter*: https://famous-trials.com/oppenheimer/2693-security-review-board-findings-recommendation-may-27-1954)

105. Hans Bethe. Quoted in Institute of Advanced Study, 'J. Robert Oppenheimer: Life, Work, and Legacy': https://ias.edu/oppenheimer-legacy (accessed 12 May 2024).

106. Fred Ribe, Letter to President Eisenhower and the AEC, 7 June 1954.

107. Quoted in Royal, p.165.

108. J. Robert Oppenheimer, Reith Lectures 1953, 'Science and the Common Understanding – Lecture 6: The Sciences and Man's Community' (BBC transmission 20 December 1953).

109. PBS, *See It Now* (5 January 1955).

110. Quoted in Peter J. Goodchild, *J. Robert Oppenheimer: 'Shatterer of Worlds'* (London: BBC Books, 1980) p.274.

111. Lyndon B. Johnson, Presentation of Fermi Award (2 December 1963).

INDEX